QUEENS OF THE RESISTANCE:
ALEXANDRIA OCASIO-CORTEZ

QUEENS OF THE RESISTANCE:

ALEXANDRIA OCASIO-CORTEZ

───────★───────

The Life, Times, and
Rise of "AOC"

───────★───────

BRENDA JONES AND KRISHAN TROTMAN

PLUME

PLUME

An imprint of Penguin Random House LLC
penguinrandomhouse.com

Copyright © 2020 by Brenda Jones and Krishan Trotman

Illustrations by Jonell Joshua
Interior Hand Lettering by Jonell Joshua and Dominique Jones

LIBRARY OF CONGRESS CATALOGING-IN-PUBLICATION DATA
has been applied for.

ISBN 9780593189856 (POB)
ISBN 9780593189894 (ebook)

Printed in the United States of America
1   3   5   7   9   10   8   6   4   2

BOOK DESIGN BY TIFFANY ESTREICHER

For Alexandria Ocasio-Cortez,
and all the Queens of the Resistance reading this

CONTENTS

III. LEADER

IV. RESISTANCE

V. QUEEN

You wanna be this Queen B
But ya can't be
That's why you're mad at me.
—Lil' Kim, "Big Momma Thang"

INTRODUCTION:
THE QUEENS OF THE
RESISTANCE SERIES

Dear Sis,

The Queens of the Resistance is a series that celebrates the life and times as well as the lessons and rise of our favorite sheroes and Queen Bees of politics. It's a celebration of the *boss*, the loud in their demands, and a rebellion against the long and tired patriarchy. They are the shining light and new face of the US government. The idea for the series began to germinate in 2016. Hillary Clinton was in the presidential race. She was top dog, Grade A. She was supposed to go all the way as the first female president. She had done everything right. In the 1960s, she switched parties when the Civil Rights movement was demonstrating that changing allegiance wasn't about betting on the winner but believing in a different vision for America's future. She married one of the most capable politicians of the twentieth century, Bill Clinton, who would eventually appoint the first Black secretaries of commerce and labor and put women and minorities in many positions of power. She was considered most likely to be president when she gave a commencement speech during her graduation from Wellesley, then went on to graduate Yale Law at the head of her class. She was the first female partner of two law firms in Arkansas; First Lady of Arkansas; First Lady of the United States—but she didn't stop there. She became the first female US senator from New York, a seat that had positioned Robert Kennedy to run for president, and one of the first female secretaries of state. She was the first woman *ever* to be nominated by a major political party to run for president. Even the political machine was oiled and greased to work in her favor. She had been generally considered one of the most qualified people ever to run for president, even by her opponents, but with all that going for her, somehow, some way, she didn't make it. *sigh* You can't get more presidential than Hillary Clinton in 2016. She had it all, even the majority of popular votes in the 2016 election.

So what happened? Ha! Every woman knows what happened! Everybody laughed at her in 1995, when she appeared on the *Today* show and attributed the chop-down of her husband to a "vast right-wing conspiracy," but she was right. Who knew that while we were enjoying the moment, the wind beneath our wings after two terms with the first Black president, a time that had left us proximal to a variety of enjoyable mini multi-cultures—sushi, guacamole, break dancing—there was a group of malcontents intent on making America great again . . . "great" like the 1940s. And that meant forcing women back into the kitchen, padlocking the door, and throwing away the key. There'd be no need to vilify female candidates with memes, negative ads, and sucker punches like the opposition had to do to Hillary Clinton; the social stigma would do all the policing and policy work needed to keep women out of the ring and out of the way, so the boyz could rule, unchecked, unaccountable, and unrestrained. "Less for you, more for me" has been a natural law in a capitalist society. It means getting rid of competition by every means necessary—deportation, mass incarceration, legislation, deprivation, deconstruction, and divestment, to name a few. Our sister Hillary was a woman who fell in the crosshairs of a right-wing machine dead set against any diversion from its outrageous plan—to stop collective action and make sure politics bends only to its will, not the people's. It didn't matter that Hillary was the smartest, the most prepared, or the first in this or that. Merit's not the point; it's compliance that matters, and Hillary was just too damn smart, too capable, too talented, for her own good. She had a vast right-wing conspiracy working against her, and they won . . . temporarily. And that's where this series begins. Queens of the Resistance is as much an ode to the women themselves as it is a celebration of a transcending political identity in America, unlike anything our history has ever shown us before.

With Love,
Brenda & Krishan

QUEENS OF THE RESISTANCE:
ALEXANDRIA OCASIO-CORTEZ

★ ★ ★ ★ ★ ★ ★ ★ ★ ★ ★ ★ ★

BORN

I wake up every day, and I'm a Puerto Rican girl from the Bronx.

—ALEXANDRIA OCASIO-CORTEZ,
THE NEW YORK TIMES

ALEXANDRIA THE GREAT!

Don't be fooled by the rocks that I got
I'm still, I'm still Jenny from the block.
—Jennifer Lopez, "Jenny from the Block"

Alexandria Ocasio-Cortez, nicknamed AOC, was born in the Bronx, pronounced "Da Bronx," also known as the Boogie-Down. It was the original settlement of a Dutch farmer named Jonas Bronck but it's since been crowned a name that has a bit more Latin flavor: the Bronx. *Está bien.* It's the only borough in New York City so dope it has a definite article before its name. (Sorry, Brooklyn!) Other things amazing that come from the Bronx: Sonia Sotomayor, KRS-One, twenty-seven baseball World Series championships, *A Bronx Tale*, Billy Joel, leather hats, and Levi's jeans with three patches.

But let's keep it real about this incredible millennial and saucy representative of District 14 of Queens and the Boogie-Down, and begin this wandering into a new outlook on politics using her own words, because if you've scoped her Insta, you know, girl, AOC is infamous for keeping it *100* and she doesn't need some dotty author's introduction. This was the queen's campaign ad that led to her election, that led to our fist emojis and praises of "*yaasss, finally*" every time she went viral taking down crooked politicians on TV, or when she appeared walking through a congressional hall in a white cape and big gold hoop earrings:

Women like me aren't supposed to run for office.

I wasn't born to a wealthy or powerful family. Mother from Puerto Rico. Dad from the Bronx. I was born in a place where your zip code determines your destiny.

My name is Alexandria Ocasio-Cortez. I'm an educator, an organizer, a working-class New Yorker. I've worked with expectant mothers, I've waited tables and led classrooms, and going into politics wasn't in the plan. But after twenty years of the same representation we have to ask: who has New York been changing for?

Every day gets harder for working families like mine to get by.

The rent gets higher, healthcare covers less, and our income stays the same. It's clear that these changes haven't been for us, and we deserve a champion.

It's time to fight for a New York that working families can afford. That's why I'm running for Congress. This race is about people versus money.

*We've got people, they've got money. It's time we ac-
knowledged that not all Democrats are the same.*

*That a Democrat who takes money, profits off foreclo-
sure, doesn't live here, doesn't send his kids to our schools,
doesn't drink our water, doesn't breathe our air cannot possibly represent us. What the Bronx and Queens needs is
Medicare for All, tuition-free public college, a federal jobs
guarantee, and criminal-justice reform.*

We can do it now.

*It doesn't take a hundred years to do this. It takes politi-
cal courage.*

How Alexandria Ocasio-Cortez went from bartender
one day to one of the youngest members of Congress ever
elected in all of American history the next is a story of
our times in politics. It is the place where politics and activism must merge. It is the catalyst to a series like the
Queens of the Resistance. Sis, it's time to put down the latte
and get your swirl on in politics no matter what your age.
Women like AOC are pulling back the curtain on patriarchy and introducing a new swag in government. She's been
a guest judge on *RuPaul's Drag Race*, for chrissakes! That's
hitting intersectionality, culture, and politics all in one
night of fabulousness. And she rented the dress, honey.
AOC is not one of these rich politicians rapping about the
poor but has never seen a broke day in her life. She has

student debt and rent-making issues like the rest of the millennials.

Politics is planning, it's strategy, it's science, it's aching feet and nonstop eighteen-hour days, but when there are mice biting at the edges of democracy, new leadership must show its face. When the country has a unified fever for change, someone like AOC appears on the scene and we pay attention—it may look like magic where we wonder, mouth agape, how in the heck did she go from the Flats Fix restaurant to *The View*? But that's the flava of a good American story, and there's a lot more to it than "pretty bartender enters ringside." It took hard work, a fierce team, and tons and tons of resistance.

Her drive to run for Congress stemmed from the absurdity of recent times that got many of us to pay attention to politics. And it's a great thing when young people get fired up to change the world.

Martin Luther King Jr., Rep. John Lewis, and even Jesus were in their youth when they wrapped their arms around a fed-up society and had the strength to pick it up. There can be a generational divide on some things, but not matters of the heart. And let's face it, AOC's a millennial who likes to dance and does facials on Insta, baby. She's not married with children; she's still adulting, up late having wine and popcorn for dinner while waiting for her boyfriend. Girl, she's like

Olivia Pope but without all the relationship drama and life-long soapbox in DC.

The beauty of AOC is not that she's any different from us, it's that finally we see faces in government that look like us. AOC's come-up was with a squad, a tribe—representatives like Ayanna Pressley, Ilhan Omar, Rashida Tlaib, and more. She and other Queens of the Resistance have had the courage to take on the huge challenge of giving a facelift to politics as we know it to get themselves elected. And now AOC continues to fight that same battle day after day in the House of Representatives. And she'll do it in a pair of Timberland boots or six-inch heels; either way, she does it with her own style. She's never anyone else but Alexandria Ocasio-Cortez. Her rise started with a response to an idea, which became a plan and birthed a strategy. She doesn't lead using a template, because that's not what has gotten her this far, sis.

But before we get to her trailblazing rise, we first have to understand where she came from. . . .

THE TENETS OF SERGIO

You are the sunshine of my life
That's why I'll always be around.
—Stevie Wonder, "You Are the Sunshine of My Life"

A s you probably know by now, when our Boricua, Alexandria Ocasio-Cortez, was born, her family resided in the Parkchester area of the Bronx. (*Boricua* means "Brave and Noble Lord." *Boriken* or *Boriquín* are the indigenous names from which *Boricua* ascended on the island of Puerto Rico. Many, many years ago before the Spanish came along with their trickery and conquered, the Boricuas ruled. **wink** Queenhood is in our Boricua's blood.)

There are many fantastical tales of wonder and enchantment that originated in the Bronx during the 1980s and '90s: *How the García Girls Lost Their Accents*, Gloria Estefan, and that of Alexandria Ocasio-Cortez, but it is Sergio Ocasio-Roman, Alexandria the Great's father, who begins this story in Parkchester.

Parkchester at one time was a large school that housed orphaned and troubled boys. In 1938, during the height of the Great Depression, the Metropolitan Life Insurance Company, then one of the biggest corporations in America, decided to diversify by investing in real estate. They built Parkchester, one of the first self-contained communities for working-class families who needed to purchase affordable property. Met Life, like many manufacturing companies at the time, built company towns. In order to make working for these companies attractive and accessible, corporations built whole towns that had housing and all the amenities people would need. It was whites-only at the time and also became a haven for WWII vets seeking a way and means for their families in return for their service to the nation. Despite change and the passage of time, it was still considered one of the most successful housing developments in New York.

This area would eventually become the neighborhood where Sergio was born on November 24, 1959, to parents Sergio Ocasio and Thamar Neirida Ocasio, who hailed from the Caribbean-blue sea of Puerto Rico.

From the time that Sergio was eleven years old to when he was twenty-one, the Bronx lost 97 percent of its buildings to fire. Bronx residents were blamed for the debacle, but actually, because property values had begun to fall, landlords found they could not sell their buildings for a profit, so they began to set their buildings on fire to collect the insurance, often in the millions of dollars. It was one of the defining periods of Sergio's life.

"I was born to a dad who was born in the South Bronx while the Bronx was burning, while landlords were committing arson to their own buildings," AOC recalled in an interview with *Vogue* magazine. "He grew up as a kid with five people in a one-bedroom apartment."

Over time, due to urban wizardry, Parkchester transformed from a moderate-income community, built to give opportunity to those seeking to own property, to a place that welcomed a more diverse community, too. And with that, a great "white flight" ensued. There began an exodus of more affluent white owners, and as economic stability declined in the South Bronx, violence and tension rose to its peak, leaving the remaining brown residents with crooked landlords and less safety.

Yet the flowers still bloomed in Parkchester.

Growing up in the Bronx in the 1960s as a Puerto Rican man with an outgrown mane and healthy mustache, Sergio was an ambitious, politically conscious young man who could both run a business during the week and roast a pig in a pit on the weekends. He loved to fish. Best of all, he used his intelligence and know-how to pull his family forward at every opportunity.

Over the course of Sergio's youth, the Puerto Rican population of New York grew to hundreds of thousands of people.

Nearly 80 percent of the Hispanic community in New York was Puerto Rican between 1970 and the early 1990s.

It's notable that Sergio Ocasio decided to become an architect, and there must have been something about the redbrick village of Parkchester that made him want to contribute. He set up his company right there in Parkchester. Kirschenbaum Ocasio-Roman Architects PC was operated out of a six-hundred-foot ground-level apartment on Archer Road. He shared the space with his business partner and six employees. Not only did they specialize in building and inspection services, they offered landscaping, lawn maintenance, engineering services, and more for Parkchester's South and North divisions. Managers and developers of low-income housing in the Bronx and Westchester County, such as Promesa, a social services company, would also commission Sergio's firm.

The media has attacked and criticized Queen AOC for stating that she and her family were poor. Oh, please! A consulting service of $65 per hour can afford you a business and a home but doesn't scream "rich"! There are many working people with homes and businesses in this nation who are only a paycheck away from "poor." Alexandria once said, "If we can acknowledge how many Americans are actually in poverty, I think that we can start to address some of the more systemic issues in our economy."

It was on a business trip to Puerto Rico where Sergio met the beautiful and marvelous Blanca Cortez, la madre de

Alexandria. According to AOC, Blanca and her family lived in poverty in Puerto Rico, and she spent much of her life raising her siblings while her own mother worked. The two were a handsome pair—Sergio's height and dark features met Blanca's petite and fair ones, and they were married in a church in Puerto Rico and then moved to the Bronx.

In 1986, Sergio bought their 725-square-foot home on Unionport Road in Parkchester, and they started a family. Their first child, Alexandria Ocasio-Cortez, came along on October 13, 1989. A few years later, a son was born, Gabriel. He calls himself "the proudest brother in the world."

Sergio was a visionary. He saw that safe and secure housing was an issue that defined the lives of the community of the South Bronx, so he'd started his architectural firm. Blanca was committed to a better life for her young family, and she helped with the household by balancing secretarial and cleaning work. Sergio and Blanca weren't rich; they were survivors.

When Alexandria was five years old, the family made the big decision to move out of Parkchester, where generations of their family still remained, to Yorktown Heights, a suburb in Westchester County, in order to put the children in a better school system. They could only afford a small house in this prosperous community. It was a little white house, just two bedrooms; one would be for Sergio and his Blanca and the other for Alexandria and Gabriel. The new home was surrounded by trees and a lawn where flowers could be planted,

and a driveway where Sergio could pull in after a long day's work. It was quiet, it was safe. It was the American dream.

Sergio's parents had pushed for his education, and now he'd do the same for their children. As AOC mentioned, she was raised in a time when your zip code determined your education, and it still does. In this case, it became a power move for Sergio to get his children out of Parkchester. Blanca was right: their kids deserved the best. He'd count pennies and make calls to his family to ask for a helping hand, if that's what it took. In typical New York "rent party" style, Sergio's aunts, uncles, and extended family chipped in to help. Getting the house was just one big push, but staying there would be a constant struggle. He summoned his Boricua bravery and challenged fate, determined to make a space where his children could thrive. Better schools and a good education was what he was betting on, along with an environment that was frankly less political and more . . . well, peaceful. Parkchester would forever be their home, it was their beginning, but it didn't need to be the only place they knew.

Think about it: the first wave of Puerto Ricans settled in the United States in 1917, with successive waves to follow in the 1930s and beyond. It was a hustle, and the sacrifice was time, exhaustion, sweat, and bone-breaking labor in exchange for the grander future it would funnel to their families. It wasn't about staying in the present, it was about the future. The language barrier made it impossible for many workers to compete for the better jobs. And the darker a person's skin was, the harder it was to succeed. Doors of opportunity were tightly closed, and a true path ahead was shielded and made difficult.

They were wrestling with racial discrimination, severe poverty, and unemployment. By the time young Sergio was of age, there was a decline in Puerto Rican migration—many returned home to their native land, where they'd struggle with finances but not acceptance.

Puerto Ricans have long marshaled political movements to address civil rights for equal access to education, employment, citizenship rights, and electoral representation. Organizers like Gilberto Gerena Valentín and Manny Diaz were key in organizing the Puerto Rican participation in the March on Washington with Martin Luther King Jr. in 1963. Valentín and Irma Vidal Santaella helped to found the National Association for Puerto Rican Civil Rights, and Santaella went on to become the first Puerto Rican woman on the New York State Supreme Court.

They organized to support the reauthorization of the Voting Rights Act of 1965. This was a crowning achievement of the Civil Rights movement, which prohibited racial discrimination in voting and outlawed many voter-suppression tactics like literacy tests. They also helped win mandates for the creation of bilingual ballots and other bilingual election materials that made multicultural representation possible at the ballot box for ethnic communities all over America. More than four thousand Puerto Ricans from New York worked in solidarity in 1968 with the Poor People's Campaign, envisioned by Dr. King with the goal of demanding that Congress create an Economic Bill of Rights for the poor.

Women also participated in activism, as around the country they formed chapters of the National Conference of Puerto Rican Women. "My aunt and my uncle were just talking last Christmas," Alexandria said in 2016, "about how they literally heard Malcolm X evangelizing on street corners. That is the institutional memory of my family and multigenerational New York families." Puerto Rican immigrants came to New York, and many moved to an area just east of Harlem, often referred to as Spanish Harlem, and the two communities developed a synergy that was especially fervent in the late twentieth century.

The Puerto Ricans got it. They were seeking liberation themselves, and they had long seen a connection between their oppression and the oppression of other people of color throughout the Americas.

Due to Black and Puerto Rican activism to ensure access to the ballot box, in the 1970s, Herman Badillo was the first Puerto Rican elected to Congress. In 1992, Nydia Velázquez became the first woman of Puerto Rican descent to be elected to Congress. The sacrifices of those who were uncomfortable, disoriented, and made to feel like they did not belong have served their successors well; they held the ladders that women like AOC and Sonia Sotomayor continue to climb.

A few high-profile Puerto Rican fly girls have included: Nydia Velázquez; Antonia Pantoja, who in 1996 was the first Puerto Rican woman to receive the Presidential Medal of Freedom, from President Bill Clinton; and Justice Sonia Sotomayor, who in 2009 became the first Latina appointed to the Supreme Court, by President Barack Obama.

Alexandria's belief in justice is an extension of her dad's belief in equality and brotherhood. She often shares the stories of when her dad invited workers from the local Dunkin' Donuts to their home. "My dad used to say that he collected people. If you didn't have a place to go to on Thanksgiving, you came to our place. We never had a table big enough to fit everyone, but we'd always have folding chairs. You'd make a plate, eat it out of your lap, and share stories." If there would be turkey for his family, there would be turkey for all. And those lessons became a foundation and key principles of AOC's. But her father wanted her to do more than strive; he also wanted her to dream.

Alexandria told *The New Yorker* about a fishing trip she went on with her dad and his buddies, and how he'd opened her eyes to the possibilities at five years old:

[There were] three burly men and a five-year-old in a sedan [on the trip] . . . One day, his buddies went to get a

beer or something, and he took me to the reflecting pool of the Washington Monument. I put my toes in the water, and suddenly the goldfish started to nibble my toes. It was a beautiful day, the sun was out, totally clear. And my dad pointed to all of it—the reflecting pool, the monuments, the Capitol, and he said, "You know, this is our government. All of this belongs to us. It belongs to you."

His inspiration made an impression upon her she would never forget. It made her feel that leadership was within her reach.

★

ZIP CODE, DA BRONX

I never had a problem showin'
y'all the real me.
—Cardi B, feat. Chance the Rapper, "Best Life"

Yorktown is forty-five miles outside of New York City in Westchester County. There's an old railroad station, built in 1877, and maybe two or three historical landmarks. Dave Matthews grew up there. There aren't many famous events or concert happenings to make it a travel destination. Let's be clear: Yorktown isn't as poppin' as the Bronx, darling, but it had a better school district. And that made it grade A to AOC's parents, as it would to many others.

In addition to a better school system, car garages, and the hope of prosperity that hung in the air of Yorktown, its canvas was predominantly white. When Alexandria started school, in her five-year-old eyes, there was no difference in skin color and hair texture from her peers that she needed to reckon with. She was who she was: little Alex Ocasio-Cortez, daughter of Sergio and Blanca. Her thick, dark locks looked different from those of her classmates. Her mother spoke Spanish, and was learning English, and her father worked incredibly hard as an architect—a prestigious job, but he was still different from the other dads.

But back in the Bronx, just down the Cross Bronx Expressway, there were dividing lines across the skyline that a five-year-old Alex could not understand yet but did notice.

As they drove into the city, the painted homes of Westchester County faded into a scale of brown apartment buildings, subway lines, and the rawest of the ghetto showed its face. Along with the trees and landscape, the faces and bodies metamorphosed. There would be more people who looked like her, who spoke the language of her mother, and there'd be lots of sound: Spanglish, hip-hop pulsating from a boom box, Funkmaster Flex or D-Nice spinning on Hot 97, and by the 2000s, reggaeton seeping out of sixth-floor windows. The summers were grueling hot in a bed of urban towers; the fire hydrants were opened with screwdrivers, and kids used them like sprinklers to play and get wet. The parks were either full of birthday parties and barbecues or empty, depending on what had transpired the night before.

The Bronx was culture and vibe heavy, while the sleepy towns of Westchester were quiet and safe. They were two worlds, and Alexandria existed in both.

Parkchester was *lit* with energy, action, and fun for a young Puerto Rican going back and forth to see her family,

but also delicate; in the shadows and crevices of the hood was a violence and chaos that brewed and showed up in the lives of her cousins and friends, too, and they lived with it every day. "Their stories are not really mine to tell," Alexandria later told *The New Yorker*, "but growing up they were wearing T-shirts with pictures of their friends who had died—and that's just scraping the surface."

As she grew, she noticed those lines weren't so invisible—there was her reality, and that of her cousins'; differences of zip code meant differences of resources. They were just as smart, just as gifted, just as full of ideas and personality as her peers in Yorktown, but society did not treat them as if their lives had the same meaning . . . and she began to wonder why. It would become so overwhelming, this blatant and unfair difference, that one day it would lead to her run for office.

She also developed a keen understanding of the poignant similarities between her hood and that of her cousins, when it came to the needs of the people and the pains of scraping by that are universal. To be sure, people who lived and worked in both neighborhoods knew the strain of having to decide whether to fix the car or risk the late payment; or the excruciating, unnerving feeling of having to correct a leaky roof or put out the funds for a pricey school trip while the family was already struggling to manage every dollar. These whispers and worries of her parents from behind closed doors was the thread between AOC's experience in York-town and that of her family in the Bronx. That fundamental unfairness taught her from the jump that even in wealthy areas, there are still people who struggle—and that wealth comes at a cost that others pay. She once said, "The thing that people don't realize is that wherever there is affluence, there's an underclass."

Moving between two worlds apart, Alexandria developed an awareness of issues in low-income communities that would propel her to *bring it* as an A-1 congresswoman.

SCHOOL DAYZ

Now, this is a story all about how
my life got flipped-turned upside down.
—DJ Jazzy Jeff & the Fresh Prince,
"Fresh Prince of Bel-Air (Theme Song)"

While living between Westchester and the Bronx gave her some real-life lessons, young Alexandria was also dedicated to learning in the classroom in Yorktown.

As a minority at a nearly all-white high school, Alexandria had often exceeded her teachers' low expectations. She was geek chic and read *The New York Times* daily, even as a teen. It was the beginning of her sense that information could be a way to fight back against the hardness of a world that could never comprehend what she had witnessed in her everyday life. She wore her difference like a badge and used it as a way to stand out from the crowd.

And stand out she did. She excelled in science, and prepared early on for a career in medicine. She was interested in health and had a natural inclination to be a healer. Similar to the way her father wanted to heal the housing blight he saw at the center of the struggle of people he loved in the South Bronx, she wanted to return her people to health and vibrancy. Her high school science teacher Michael Blueglass later recounted to *The New York Times*, "She was interested in research to help people in all areas, including developing nations, not just for the people with money."

As early as ninth grade, Alexandria participated in the Great Debate, a conference where 150–300 students would gather to discuss Latinx issues with the goal of designing new, innovative road maps for social change. She honed her skill in speaking truth to power at the National Institutes of Health's College Ready Network, where she was mentored by some of the premier biological researchers in the world. She also participated in the Lorenzo de Zavala Youth Legislative Session, a youth government that teaches its students how to develop their own community policies and manage large organizations. It's hosted by the National Hispanic Institute, a nonprofit organization that fosters future Latinx community leaders. It convenes students from more than twenty-five states and four Latin American countries. Once she went to college, she served as the Lorenzo de Zavala Youth Legislative Session's secretary of state.

MEANWHILE, HER STUDIOUS, inquisitive nature led her to develop a research study with her mentors at the NIH College Ready Network and enter it into a science fair in 2007, when she was a senior in high school. The Intel International Science and Engineering Fair is no rinky-dink high school gig: it's the largest precollege exhibition of scientific research in the world. Alexandria felt that her research offered great insight on a compound that may help regenerate the cells of a simple organism, roundworms to be exact, after they had been exposed to damage caused by oxidative stress.

So, hold on here, sis, because this is some complex stuff, and it gets kind of deep. "Free radicals" is a term thrown around a lot in health-food circles that many researchers think might be one of the causes of diseases like cancer. Basically, free radicals are like rogue cells that are unstable, so they are looking for other cells to join up with. The first problem is that when they join with healthy cells they can weaken the vitality of those cells. The second problem is that they can cause a lot of damage because they like to pair up a lot, but they are always bringing bad vibes with them. It's kinda like that guy who always wants to hang out with the baes, but instead of just chillaxing and enjoying himself, he ends up bringing the baes around him down—he's just negative energy. Then they get stressed out and want him to leave. On a cellular level, that chain reaction is called oxidative stress, and oxygen issues are one reason people suffer from chronic illness.

So check this out. Alexandria did a test to see whether a certain chemical compound would have a positive effect on cells (baes) that were having a hard time getting rid of this dude at the party. She introduced an antioxidant for the experiment, and the results were promising enough to indicate it might work in more complex organisms than the roundworms she used. Alexandria knew she wanted to be some kind of healer, so the most obvious choice of profession for someone with her brains and her concern for other people was medicine. Little did she know, she would one day be involved in devising treatment plans all right—but not just for individual people, for an entire society.

Okay, so even if it's totally incomprehensible to you what AOC's experiment was, either because you empathized with the dude over the baes in the analogy or because science just isn't your thing, you have to admit, that's pretty impressive. Well, the judges at this world-renowned science fair thought Alexandria's research was pretty impressive too: she won second place. A little girl from the South Bronx killed it in a science fair where she beat out all but one of the other geeks from around the world, usually guys, who are expected to be the smartest ones in the room. *Not!*

Still, it wasn't a total victory. Alexandria said that when she asked around among the doctors at Mount Sinai Hospital in New York, where she conducted her experiment, why there were not more scientists pursuing the promise of these kinds of results, she was told it was because pharmaceutical companies had discouraged researchers from doing it. Years, later, when AOC made it to Congress, Maya Ajmera, president and CEO of the Society for Science & the Public, and publisher of *Science News*, later said, "We expect that the lessons she learned during ISEF—the importance of evidence-based science, clear communication and team work—will translate well in her work on Capitol Hill." And in fact it has.

An especially neat thing about this whole science-fair experience is that the second-place winner of the competition gets a star—not a star on the Hollywood Walk of Fame, but an actual star in the sky—named after them. Her star, well, actually an asteroid, was named by MIT's Lincoln Laboratory: it's called 23238 Ocasio-Cortez. How many people in high school can say they have a star in the universe named after them? Our queen was killing it already at the age of seventeen.

AFTER CONDUCTING THIS rewarding research at a top-notch medical hospital like Mount Sinai, Alexandria was well on her way to a career in medicine. However, equal to her

passion for science, in high school, was her urgency to challenge the ideas of people around her. This drive manifested in her Great Debate experience, and it would continue to be a major focus in her life. After high school graduation she'd go on to become the educational director at the National Hispanic Institute. In 2017 she was awarded the NHI Person of the Year.

NHI founder and president Ernesto Nieto stated, "Alex symbolizes the new emerging Latina—bold and courageous, well-educated and forward-thinking, contemporary with her ideas and views, and unafraid of challenges . . . It's her character, her determination to succeed, and her community vision that makes the difference. It was there when she first joined us at sixteen years of age and continues today. Alex is among the rising difference makers who are destined to impact our future as a country."

IT WAS NO surprise that our highly praised, award-winning queen would go to a great college; though money was still tight at home, scholarships, including a John F. Lopez Internship from the National Hispanic Institute, and student loans helped. She enrolled at Boston University in a premed program.

As a freshman, she participated in a study-abroad program in Niger, West Africa, a country stricken with poverty that involved food and water shortages, where one in five children dies of starvation. She volunteered at a maternity clinic on the outskirts of its capital city, Niamey, on the banks of the Niger River, helping midwives deliver babies. In a 2019 interview with *Bon Appétit*, Alexandria spoke of the extreme poverty she witnessed, including poor medical facilities for the women she served. The babies were being born on steel tables, and there were a tragic number of stillbirths. "The reason the child has passed was very preventable . . . This child's life was literally decided because of where it was born," she wrote in one instance.

Alexandria had personally known the impact of inequality from her life in the Bronx, but to see it through an international lens . . . it affected her. The Bronx is New York's poorest borough, with a poverty rate of 30 percent and more than half of the residents earning under $40,000 a year. That doesn't sound too bad, right? But juxtapose that against the average $2,000 rent for a one-bedroom apartment and the economics look bleak. She had walked these delicate lines her entire life, but nothing compared to what she saw in Niger. Nevertheless, it was somehow familiar.

When Alexandria returned to Boston University, she changed her major to economics and international relations. She realized how much health and economics went hand in hand. She herself had contracted malaria in Niger. "In the developing world, malaria is an economic disease. It's a disease that impacts so many people as to be actually impacting national GDP, so I started thinking about these health issues as more macroeconomic public-policy issues." The more she connected with her experience in the Sahara, the closer she came to a new calling.

She was activated, graduated with honors in May 2011, and the AOC prescription for social change was birthed. Delivering babies for the love of humanity was a great profession, but if those babies couldn't be assured of equal access to healthcare, or even survival, then there was a much larger problem that needed to be fixed.

There comes a time in every queen's life where she must step out of the background and into the light. A time when she must make a choice to mount her throne.

Can This Be the Next Great Generation?

Yes. Of course it can. Greatness has never been a result of circumstance or fortune. It is not an inherited trait or function of destiny. Greatness dresses in humble clothes. Emerging from tested integrity, unwavering belief, and unshakeable commitment. Greatness is the long haul . . . [Perhaps a more pressing question] is how can we be great, and it seems as though the first step is a choice. King made a conscious decision at Morehouse, he leaned his study toward medicine and law. It wasn't until his senior year of college that he decided to commit himself to ministry. In his own words, "as a young man with most of my life ahead of me I decided early to give my life to something eternal and absolute." This generation does not consist of a people between the ages of eighteen and thirty-five. This generation consists of all people who choose to be young at this time. It is a much smaller group, as they say it is far more work to curse the rain as it is to sow a seed; giving up is easy. It is living out our imaginations that takes work. But to live in that world is to be young. And like greatness the route to youth is not a circumstance but a choice. There are no chosen ones; there are only those who choose. It is never too late. We can choose to be great . . . We must choose to be whole in our commitment and fresh in our thoughts . . . [Whatever we do] must be done in the likeness of our own beliefs, as a reflection of our own greatness . . . A light of greatness is equal to the sum of many days of greatness. So every day we must ask ourselves, *Today, how will I be great? Tomorrow, how will I be great? In this very moment, how am I being great?*

—*Excerpt from AOC's speech at Boston University, 2011*

★ ★ ★ ★ ★ ★ ★ ★ ★ ★ ★ ★ ★

WOMAN

They'll tell you
you're too loud, that
you need to wait
your turn and ask
the right people for
permission. Do it
anyway.

—AOC, ON TWITTER

TO DREAM THE IMPOSSIBLE DREAM

The moment you own it
You better never let it go.
—Eminem, "Lose Yourself"

Financial struggle is as much a part of the cities and streets as the American dream, and Alexandria Ocasio-Cortez has never forgotten the sacrifices that her parents made throughout her childhood to make ends meet.

So she started working at a young age. One of her first jobs, back when she was about fifteen years old, was working in an Irish pub as a hostess to pay for her extracurricular activities. In the Cortez home, money was in a constant sprint to catch up with the bills no matter how hard Sergio and Blanca worked. Debt eats fast, and as the bills kept coming each month, the mortgage was in trouble more than once. The American dream looked more like a constant struggle than a happy ending. Sacrifices were made, but they at least had their home and each other, and with a little hard work, they could prosper.

Sis, this is what many Americans are striving for. AOC is a real one because she understands firsthand that the American dream isn't some rich man's ideology but in fact it's the dream of survival—one that's dependent on a culture and a government that encourages us to keep rising up, generation upon generation. Whether you're a janitor or a fashion designer, an architect or a hostess, the attainment of more ought to be possible. Alexandria's story is our own, and this is why she fights.

But things would take a turn for the worst in September 2008 when, in the thick of the financial crisis that was sparked by the subprime mortgage collapse, Sergio Ocasio-Roman passed away. Alex was nineteen years old, just starting out as a sophomore in college. Sergio was only forty-eight years old, overcome with an unusual form of lung cancer. He had been diagnosed when Alexandria was sixteen, and the family had done all they could manage for those three years with healthcare and medical bills, yet still he slipped away. His last words would forever hold a place in her heart and become her calling card to America. She told *Time*, "I didn't know that it was going to be the last time that I talked to my dad, but toward the end of our interaction, I started to feel like it was . . . I said good-bye but I think he knew I knew. And so I started to leave, and he kind of hollered out, and I turned around in the doorframe, and he said, 'Hey, make me proud.'"

AFTER HIS DEATH, suddenly things were very different for Alexandria. The year before, she had just entered Boston University. Now she was back, and her GPA skyrocketed; she was on a mission to fulfill her father's words. She was entering a new phase. The death of a parent is often a loss of innocence, and AOC was forced to see many things in a new light, including the importance of doing good and making a lasting, positive impact on the world. She had always wanted to make the world a better place, but now that focus had shifted. She changed majors from biochemistry to economics and international relations and got an internship in Sen. Ted Kennedy's Boston office, her first real-life brush with national politics.

Not only did her life change in terms of her professional aspirations and how her eyes now saw the ever-changing world, but it also changed at home. Sergio had been the breadwinner of the family, without him they had to look at security differently, and they were economically vulnerable. She learned quickly how fast that rug could be pulled from under a person's feet. Suddenly and swiftly, one of her greatest loves had been swept away, and it left an insurmountable hole in her heart that could never be filled. Even worse, that deep personal grief was compounded by a newly intensified struggle of financial responsibility on her and her mom. She later described those times: "My mother was done. My brother was lost. I took it hard, too, but I channeled it into my studies. That's how I dealt with it. I was home for a week and went right back to school."

Sergio had been one of those men who was ambitious as much for himself as he was for his children. He pushed them to achieve. Alexandria's brother, Gabriel, has said that he grew up sometimes bristling at his father's prodding, but felt his father saw something in him that he was not able to see in himself, until long after Sergio was gone. Alexandria always had a taste of nerd chic and was a daddy's girl. When he pushed, she just worked harder. Her father, she has said, "knew my soul better than anyone on this planet."

He would be so proud of the Alexandria Ocasio-Cortez we celebrate today, her willingness to stand against narrow-minded politicians as a young millennial woman of color and fight for the rights of people of color, for the love and protection of the environment and Medicare for All. She knows the government should look like her and represent the voice of a people still fighting to be seen and heard, but more importantly, have their needs met in policy and legislation, such as immigration rights, housing, and police reform, to be sure they are given a shot at generational success and not just shot with a list of generational curses. With a woman like AOC taking up a seat in government, especially on committees like the House Financial Services Committee, alongside other queens like Maxine Waters, and the House Committee on Oversight and Reform, there would be progress.

BUT FOR NOW, our queen was still nineteen years old and in a dire situation, along with many other people in this country. The 2008 recession was the worst economic downfall since the Great Depression of 1929. Unemployment was at a record high, millions of people lost their homes, and the Cortez women had to figure out how to make their way while dealing with their grief. They struggled to keep their home. Housing prices fell due to a subprime mortgage crisis driven by greedy, wealthy people at the top of the economic pyramid. People making $35,000 per year were suddenly getting $400,000 mortgages they could never pay off, with wildly spiraling interest rates. You know the story.

In this tumultuous environment, Alexandria and Blanca had to fight back against the circumstances. Like many middle-class families, they had neither insurance or stocks, nor the leisure and luck of an inheritance to fall back on. These women were going to have to pull up their sleeves and claw their way out of it, and that's just what they did. Even before the economy crashed and Sergio passed away, there had barely been enough for healthcare. Sergio had put everything into their home, the business, and providing from day to day. There was never enough for a safety net, only survival.

During all this, Alexandria was in the midst of college deadlines in Boston, and she'd go on to graduate cum laude. But when she was home in New York, she cleaned homes with her mom to make money. She had to help her mom pay the mortgage, and save her father's legacy. And the phone calls from the banks and bill collectors only added pressure, and her grief only made it harder. Still Blanca and AOC pushed through it. They cleaned the homes of their neighbors to keep their own. It was the house that Sergio had worked so hard to maintain, the new beginning they had fought for. Blanca was a single parent now—a widow—and she'd make a way. She'd drive a bus. She'd clean a house. She'd answer phones in secretarial jobs. She'd do whatever it took to make ends meet.

MOJITOS 'N' POLITICOS

Say what you wanna say
And let the words fall out
Honestly, I wanna see you be brave.
—Sara Bareilles, "Brave"

After college, Alexandria started working as a bartender at Flats Fix, a taqueria in the heart of New York in Union Square and the East Village, because like most college grads who are mentally drained, financially depleted, and trying to get their heads back on straight, she knew that she just wasn't inspired to go into a profession in economics yet. She could easily have gotten a cushy Wall Street job, but she later told *Vogue*, "I just physically couldn't do it. I knew it would kill me on the inside. It's not like I felt enlightened waiting tables, but I knew I couldn't do the other thing." She wanted to be in a profession where she could help people but still didn't have a handle yet on how she'd do that with an economics degree.

She did know, girl, that she had to work—bartending, cleaning homes with her mom, whatever it took for their survival in New York and in the fight to keep their home. So she found herself at Flats Fix, doing something she enjoyed, flipping añejo old-fashioned, shots of Patrón, and Mayan mules and engaging with people in a different kind of sociology. *snap, snap*

At the bar, she was the friendly, kind bartender whom they called Sandy, and would spend the afternoon talking politics with the lunch crowd. She had volunteered on the Bernie Sanders campaign and now was perplexed about how the country could elect the wacky and potentially dangerous Donald Trump. She had heard about the protests by Native Americans at the Standing Rock Sioux Reservation in North Dakota, and she raised money at the bar for a road trip there. One taco regular, Scott Starrett, told *Insider* magazine that he lent her his camera to document the event.

As a bartender, she worked in an industry known for ten- to fifteen-hour shifts full of prep work, late-night cleanups, and catering to the demands of the customers, and she'd take just as much of the knowledge she learned there about hard work and the working class with her to Congress as what she learned in any economics class.

She told *Insider*, "I got really, really, really good at listening to people, and I got really good at understanding people's needs, beyond just food and drink."

The restaurant was founded on blue-collar labor hustle, too, having once been a tire shop where the owner's wife would prepare delicious tacos in the back. It's still there in NYC, a space the size of a four-car garage transformed by a twenty-five-foot mahogany bar and adorned with Mexican art inspired by the likes of Frida Kahlo, with skeletal masks shrouded in flowers. Surfboards, loud people, and posters, the room is full in every way, and Alexandria juggled her day-to-day life there and her new adventure as she entered politics.

Starting at the top of 2017, for about a year, her daily schedule would include racing between Flats Fix and the Bronx, an hour-long commute; talking to people who came through Flats Fix, serving them drinks, and showing them a good time; and then going over to talk to voters at the neighborhood grocery stores and churches. At one point she posted a picture of sizable holes in her shoes, damaged from the crazy amount of walking she'd been doing on a daily basis, through sun, snow, and sleet, sis.

In the middle of slow-smoked brisket tacos and Coronas, the beltway of Flats Fix is where AOC was schooled. She told *Rolling Stone*, "The thing that people don't understand about restaurants is that they're one of the most political environments. You're shoulder-to-shoulder with immigrants. You're at one of the nexuses of income inequality. Your hourly wage is even less than the minimum wage. You're working for tips. You're getting sexually harassed. You see how our food is processed and handled. You see how the

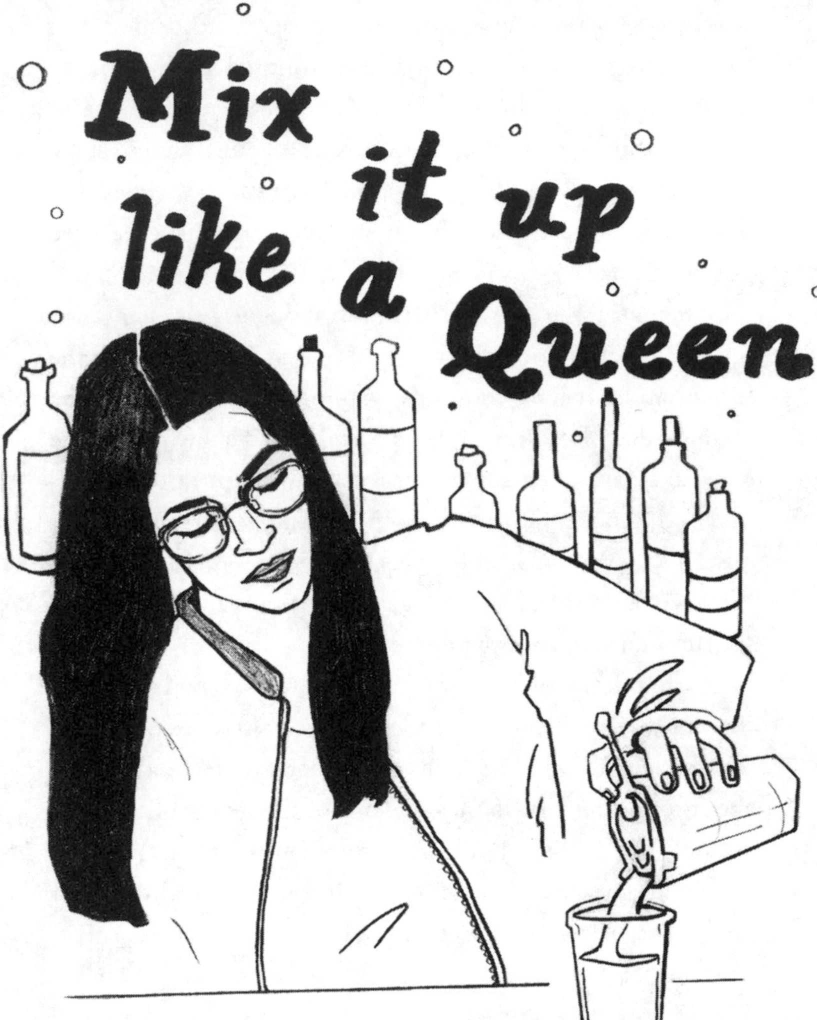
Mix it up like a Queen

prices of things change. It was a very galvanizing political experience for me."

Alexandria had a view from inside the kitchen—largely populated by immigrants of Mexican descent, underpaid, surviving, and raising families on about $5 per hour plus tips (the tipped minimum wage went up in 2016). It was also yet another life experience for her that drove home the message that the politics really is personal. "Many members of Congress were born into wealth, or they grew up around it," she later told *Bon Appétit*. "How can you legislate a better life for working people if you've never been a working person? Try living with the anxiety of not having health insurance for three years when your tooth starts to hurt. It's this existential dread. I have that perspective. I [understand] what's happening electorally because I have experienced it myself."

★

THE STANDING ROCK

Time to save the world
Where in the world is all the time?
—Erykah Badu, "Didn't Cha Know"

Sis, I know your parents have marveled since your kindergarten years about what you'd do with your life, who you'd become. But no one knows. Sometimes the non-plan ends up being the most rewarding plan. Just look at AOC, who went from a premed student to a bartender to a lawmaker by seeking out places where she could do some good, and it's how she found her way into politics.

"I first started considering running for Congress, actually, at Standing Rock in North Dakota," Alexandria Ocasio-Cortez said in 2018. "It was really from that crucible of activism where I saw people putting their lives on the line . . . for people they've never met and have never known. When I saw that, I knew that I had to do something more."

In August of that year a group of thirty-eight people, mostly teenagers, from the Great Sioux Nation—a confederation of the Lakota, Dakota, and Nakota Native peoples—set out to run two thousand miles from Standing Rock Reservation in North Dakota all the way to Washington, DC. They were determined to deliver a petition to the US Army Corps of Engineers to stop the building of a massive oil pipeline meant to cross the Missouri River that would jeopardize the purity of the reservation's sole source of water and even violate ancestral burial sites. The Lakota drafted a petition and received 157,000 signatures, including those of some celebrities like Leonardo DiCaprio, Shailene Woodley, and Jason Momoa. (We love when people *pull up*, as you put it, Rihanna!)

The Dakota Access Pipeline would carry oil in a 1,172-mile underground route from North Dakota to Illinois at a rate of 570,000 barrels per day.

The Lakota's position was that the pipeline could be dug in a way that would avoid the reservation and not put their homes, their families, their land, and their way of life in jeopardy.

Sioux Nation families were deeply concerned that if an accident were to happen, and chances were it would, or if leakage occurred that was not detected initially, their only source of water would be contaminated, leaving their homeland uninhabitable.

Earlier that year, after the Standing Rock community learned that Energy Transfer Partners (ETP) had plans to create the Dakota Access Pipeline that would run from the fracked Bakken oil fields in western North Dakota all the way to southern Illinois, the young people of Standing Rock organized a grassroots movement called ReZpect Our Water. They vowed to remain in the encampment that blocked the construction until the pipeline project was "killed." They created a Seven Council camp, with more than five dozen Native tribes represented. They established a water protectors' camp that directed action and centralized spiritual protection of the water, culture, and the independent sovereignty of the indigenous people.

By September the encampments had grown, and more than three hundred Native tribes were represented, three thousand to four thousand water protectors were lodged in the pipeline construction areas, and several thousand more would join them on the weekends.

AOC had ridden up with some friends to Standing Rock in December 2016 to participate in the protest after the Army Corps of Engineers began digging the pipeline 1.5 miles upstream from Standing Rock Reservation. They had quietly granted a permit to ETP, in a streamlined process that avoided the ordinary public comment period. Sis, the protesters had been trying to reach out to the Army Corps of Engineers since 2014 but to no avail. Now they were supposed to feel comforted by an Army Corps environmental impact statement that had been ordered by three federal agencies due to legal actions by Native lawyers, which was issued that spring of 2016 and determined there would be no impact on the community. However, the report turned a blind eye to the proximity of the pipeline—less than two miles from their community.

ETP quietly purchased the land where some of the water protectors were located and moved construction equipment onto it, ignoring the cries of the protesters. Protesters chained themselves to construction equipment, and a private security force moved in to forcibly arrest them. One hundred and eighty people were arrested.

The water protectors remained at Standing Rock for many months; even into the dead of winter hundreds were still left.

Finally, in December 2016, President Barack Obama blocked ETP's easement to cross the Missouri River about a half mile upstream from the Standing Rock Reservation. Construction stopped!

At a Martin Luther King Jr. celebration in 2017, AOC told the Park Avenue Christian Church, "[Standing Rock] was truly one of the most spiritually transformative experiences of my life. I remember leaving that camp and thinking, *Lord, just do with me what you will. Allow me to be a vessel.* And [when] I was driving off the camp I got an email asking if I would consider a run for Congress. I felt the spirit of that preparation. I felt like this was my charge. And I didn't know if I would win. I didn't know if I would lose. I knew I was being told to run."

It was the first time in many years that a variety of Native tribes had come together as one to demonstrate their solidarity and to share their way of life with one another and their visitors. It was these stories of infringement, oppression, and the audacity to persevere through it all that inspired Alexandria Ocasio-Cortez and hundreds of protesters to stand with the people of Standing Rock.

At Standing Rock, the indomitable AOC was birthed. She witnessed the struggle of people fighting against corporate and governmental forces that had manipulated the power of the police and the media, and called in their helicopters and dogs to enforce their will even when it was wrong. Something had changed inside her. She felt she could not remain silent; she also had learned a great lesson about change. A lesson that is not easy to learn or popular to believe: change is possible. She had to take action, and it was while she was at Standing Rock that the Brand New Congress initiative phoned her, and she answered the calling.

Unfortunately, in February 2017, President Trump approved the construction of the pipeline, which began again. But Standing Rock had still served its purpose as an inspiration to many . . . and as for Trump, he would soon have to answer to Rep. Ocasio-Cortez.

★

"I AM RUNNING FROM THE BOTTOM"

I did not come to play with you . . .
I came to slay.
—Beyoncé, "Formation"

After his 2016 loss, a few Bernie Sanders staffers started the organization Brand New Congress (BNC) with the aim of recruiting candidates who were not your typical politicians, aka old white men—like Bernie, ha! But to AOC and BNC, the soul of Bernie's movement represented the change that needed to take place. First of all, Bernie's from Brooklyn and has the accent to prove it—he's down with the revolution, calls himself an independent, and does not necessarily feel the need or pressure to lace himself up with others in the old guard—he's about everything that makes Alexandria Ocasio-Cortez's heart sing. He's not afraid to stand his ground about Medicare for All—and whoeva's mad about it should just feel the Bern, baby. He's got a helluva millennial army behind him (come on, he had Public Enemy at his 2020 campaign and sported the Flavor Flav clock—major swag!), and one of those young members following him in 2016 was Alexandria Ocasio-Cortez.

She'd stuff envelopes, knock on doors throughout New York, and do whatever she could to fight along with Sanders for what his camp described as "a Future to Believe In." Unfortunately, when he didn't win the primary, it was a sad day. A time that left a deep ache and hunger for the hope that the Bern had bestowed, which, unbeknownst to AOC, that same achy need for change would lead right back to her. According to the members of Brand New Congress, and the influence of Bernie's progressive ideas, the movement he started needed to be continued . . . and all throughout the federal government, not just in the White House.

The goal was to create a new wave, a blue shift, of progressive politics in Congress, helmed by unapologetic members, who had lived out some of the hot-button issues the progressive movement advocated for. The new Congress would look like politicians who had real stories of their own, those who had experienced the trials of having no health insurance or who had come from working-class families. Since destiny wasn't bringing in any qualified recipients herself, Brand New Congress sent out a call to action. They started, naturally, with young people who had volunteered on Bernie's 2016 presidential campaign—people like Alexandria.

They used a Bernie Sanders template to organize a campaign—their candidates would refuse to accept financial backing from big corporations so there would be no obligation to return the favor in office. Nope, there would be no more rule following. Playground politics and practices, where the business bullies wielded their financial power to reign, were *over*, sis. The change would be so deep that it would present like politics unlike it had ever been seen before—brown, black, and female. It was time to change the face of politics, and that new face would look like the real America. Real people were those who'd gone to work every day, who sometimes struggled with their finances, and maybe even a few who knew how to twerk to Cardi B. People who had lived experiences that would command better legislation for everyday people, and not just the money boys who were looking down from above the glass ceiling.

It would be a new paradigm where the government now would be modeled after its constituents. The unwealthy and unconnected would run the House and the Senate and be allies for the working and middle class. It would demonstrate what progressive really looked like, and make history. This was the dream going in, and it was beginning to come true.

They wanted new candidates in all the Democratic seats. Barack Obama had already been held back by the white male patriarchy that had pinned him up against a wall. The Brand New Congress were planning ahead for the next election, to put more incumbents on the other side of that wall, align the soldiers to be ready to go out. As millennials, their generation had not been alive for World War I, World War II, Vietnam, or much of the Cold War, but they had seen a hellfire occur in the White House that would only get worse. Obama managed to accomplish a lot and take healthcare to the next level, but the GOP tied his hands and refused to work with him, and then put a bully in the White House after him.

It was Saikat Chakrabarti, who would become Alexandria's first chief of staff, and Corbin Trent, her communications director, who began soliciting names for those working-class people who would take a chance and run against the top dogs. The organization announced their initiative on MSNBC's *Rachel Maddow Show* and received more than eleven thousand applicants.

One letter came from Gabriel Ocasio-Cortez, Alexandria's little brother. He asked his sister if she wanted to do it, and she said yes. Sometimes we have only a small lens or limited scope into our own greatness, whereas our family, friends, and colleagues can see it clearer than we do.

Remember, Alexandria had been at Standing Rock and was already fired up with inspiration. "I saw how a corporation had literally militarized itself against the American people."

Then she got the call. "Will you run for Congress in New York's Fourteenth District?" was the question asked. Brand New Congress wanted to meet with her.

Alexandria may not have even thought to nominate herself. Had she thought about it? Maybe. But it just hadn't seemed like a realistic idea for her, which is why many people don't go for it. (Go for it!) "I felt like the only way to effectively run for office is if you had access to a lot of wealth, high social influence, a lot of high dynastic power, and I knew that I didn't have any of those things. I counted out that possibility because I felt that possibility had counted out me," she told *The Cut*. But her brother didn't count her out. He was twenty-six now and had heard his sister speak formally, debating since high school, and he saw her passion for politics at kitchen-table discussions throughout their childhood. Her dedication to advocate for an idea was admirable, when she set out with her spiral notebook and pen, the power of her delivery in any matter would be effective. He knew exactly who his big sister could be.

Alexandra Rojas, a former member of the Brand New Congress would tell *Time*, "We looked at the brother telling the story of a sister who wasn't a giant nonprofit executive, she didn't go work on the Hill for 10 years . . . She was someone who watched her family struggle through the financial crisis."

Her first call from the Brand New Congress was informational. They wanted to know her story, hmmm. Not just her time in Yorktown, where her family had moved when she was small, but her life growing up in the Bronx before that. They also wanted to hear more about her role in campaigns for Ted Kennedy, for whom she'd interned, and Bernie Sanders. That call would be followed by more intense preparation calls. It was a necessity; she needed to be groomed to take on a candidate like the incumbent, Rep. Joseph Crowley, who was one of the highest-ranking Democrats in the House of Representatives. There would be weeks and weeks of calls, video chats, and team meetings. Every step had to be purposeful. She had to be ready.

They teamed with another group, Justice Democrats, for media training. She was trained on how to conduct herself with the media and coached on policy. Her debate tactics, which had been put to much different use back in high school, needed to be strengthened and honed. Living-room speeches were rehearsed over and over again. She was well spoken, but she had to be polished.

Quickly this preparation became her life.

Over the course of the entire year, after bartending for long hours at Flats Fix, Alexandria and her team of volunteers would visit 120,000 homes campaigning. After a full day of taking orders, running credit cards, dodging shade, and throwing high fives to customers, Alexandria would throw on her black blazer like a reverse Clark Kent and turn into Superwoman, zipping through the streets of New York, hopping on the 7 train and the Q and then the bus to campaign in her district. Unlike other politicians who learn about their constituents from their data, AOC spent many months and years working and walking among them, honey.

They'd make 170,000 phone calls and send 120,000 text messages in total. They joined forces with local organizations and chapters of Black Lives Matter, the Bronx Progressives, the Jackson Heights Beautification Group, the 7 Train Coalition, and Queens Neighborhoods United. One of the key organizations was the Democratic Socialists of America, who endorsed her in April 2018.

Things wouldn't be done the old way; there would be a new way, and this group, along with Alexandria, decided to figure out how. She would not only work in politics, she would be incomparable. There would be no substitute.

At twenty-seven, she'd be the symbol of unstoppable progress.

Her campaign outlined their biggest objectives: a universal jobs guarantee, the abolishment of the Immigration and Customs Enforcement Agency (ICE), and tuition-free public college.

Too many Americans were living paycheck to paycheck, and this political newbie would be someone in the House who would give them a loud and unapologetic voice. AOC's creed was: "no person should be too poor to live."

In February 2018, Alexandria quit her job at Flats Fix. Chakrabarti moved back to New York full-time from Knoxville, Tennessee, to co-chair the campaign, and sleeping on his couch would be Corbin, who left behind his family and food-truck business in Tennessee for their vision.

⭐

VOTE FOR/ *VOTA POR*
ALEXANDRIA! OCASIO! CORTEZ!

You can get with this, or you can get with that
I think you'll get with this, for this is where it's at.
—Black Sheep, "The Choice Is Yours"

W E DID IT. This Bronx girl is running for CON-GRESS! 💀 " was the tweet on April 13, 2018, to announce Alexandria Ocasio-Cortez's official run for Congress. It was followed with her cab ride to the Board of Elections with more than 5,400 signatures from registered Democrats in New York's fourteenth District. Her tweet:

- FIRST NY-14 primary in 14 years

- FIRST Democrat to make it to the NY-14 ballot with 100% volunteer effort (no hired guns)

- ONLY Democrat to run with NO LOBBYIST 💰. That means no developer money driving up rents!

- ONLY person of color to run for NY-14 in a generation (our community is 70% PoC!)

AOC was not a traditional candidate, no ma'am, and she was not running a traditional campaign. The people in the 14th District were in awe when suddenly in the windows of bodegas and Laundromats appeared these posters of a young *bonita* running for Congress. *Say whaa?* The posters were printed on bright-blue paper in bubble letters with stars and text in both English and Spanish, celebrating her heritage. This doe-eyed young woman with a low bun in her hair gazing toward the sky in a symbolic expression of hope for the future was running against Rep. Joe Crowley, a fifty-six-year-old white guy. *Say whaa?*

Meanwhile, everyone on the scene knew who Crowley was. He was the House Democratic Caucus chair (which ranked him behind only the conference chair, minority whip, and minority leader in the House caucus), and was being groomed to take on a leadership role as Speaker of the House, as Nancy Pelosi's successor. Whoa, Queen of the Resistance Pelosi is a fierce act to follow, so this dude must have been substantial, beloved, incredible. *Eeek.* How was AOC going to win this, sis?

But wait, there's more. He was a member of the powerful Ways and Means Committee, and an Irish American native New Yorker. Nothing says badass like being a New Yorker, but so was AOC. He had been in Congress for almost twenty years, so there was the esteem and influence, and about half of that time he had been representing the 14th District, and in the last election had won with 74 percent of the vote. Okay, this was . . . an issue. . . . *concerned eyebrows*

The endorsements were also, uh, pretty stacked in his favor. Here's a "quick" rundown. He was endorsed by many unions, the police, Planned Parenthood, NARAL Pro-Choice America, and the Women's Equality Party. He was also endorsed by four state senators and eleven members of the state assembly, the Bronx and Queens borough presidents, seven New York City councilmen, governor of New York Andrew Cuomo, five members of the House representing New York, and three other members of the House. He was endorsed by the Stonewall Democrats, the Human Rights Campaign, and even the Himalayan Democratic Club (*what!!!*) as well as the Jackson Heights Indian Merchants Association. Dang, the list was straight-up impressive, and it looked like the young newbie should go back home and *sit down*.

So, sis, how could she have possibly in this lifetime won? *Ooooh, it gets juicy.*

First of all, the House was scared and paranoid about new rookies coming in and talking revolutionary ideas like Medicare for All instead of appealing to the white, racist base that had gotten Trump elected and had sent the nation into chaos. Everything would be on the line in 2020, and they did not want to split the Democratic vote, so Crowley had all the help in the world from the Democratic establishment. So, again, how could he lose this race to a twenty-seven-year-old with no experience?

Well, the truth is that despite her opponent's long résumé, AOC was welcomed by the community like the Temptations' sunshine on a cloudy day. In 2018, Crowley's district had the second highest number of foreign-born residents in the state, the third highest number of Latino residents out of the twenty-seven districts in the state, and the fourth highest Asian population. The district was becoming more and more minority-based. Crowley's long and consistent reign as their representative had helped him maintain political clout, but this growing minority was starting to think, in the words of the queen Janet Jackson, *What have you done for me lately*?

Crowley was a little out of touch with their version of the American dream—yes, he had grown up in New York but he hadn't repped a Boogie-Down or Queens lifestyle in ages. It's like when Jay-Z goes back to Brooklyn. He can send over soundtracks but these days, boo, he's lunching with David Letterman on *My Next Guest* and rapping about fine wine, "Y'all [bleep] acting way too tough / Throw on a suit get it tapered up."

Not that Jay-Z is necessarily out of touch—he's an evolved king of hip-hop actually—but you get the idea. Crowley had definitely lost his handle on his district. Especially in the divisive times when his largely immigrant community was being portrayed as villains and targeted by the president on a national platform. The subtext of the election gave Alexandria a definite advantage—as a young, working-class woman of color, she looked and sounded like, and not to mention *understood*, the future of the district.

But beyond this, Crowley decided to run *against Trump*, instead of running *for the people* in his district. He invested most of his campaign funds in ads highlighting his anti-Trump agenda. In 2017 he introduced a bill to give citizenship to undocumented workers who'd helped to clean up and recover after 9/11, and was a vocal critic of Trump's Mexican border wall. He had already started to have small meetings with lawmakers about becoming Speaker, and thought everything was all set for his new seat (though Queen of the Resistance Pelosi was not going anywhere just yet, Crowley. *Oh puhlease!*). The blinding white male privilege was apparent, though things did seem to be lining up for him. . . .

Except that this time, he had a charismatic challenger. In a sharp contrast to Crowley's approach, Alexandria's message to the people of the district was clear. She was one of them. Again, her campaign championed her identity, and in a spirited movie poster–like design, it seemed to unapologetically celebrate being Latinx. Her campaign brand avoided that stale red, white, and blue flag, but she was also filled with some JLo flava, smart, fun, and bold.

Her campaign was multicultural inside and out. She wasn't cashing in on the optics of diversity. Her heritage wouldn't be used for the sake of PR. Her hiring reflected the diversity of the boroughs she was running to represent too: her campaign manager and first chief of staff, Saikat Chakrabarti, was Indian; Donnie Whitehead and Jo-Ann Floyd-Whitehead, who helped her on the campaign, were revered longtime African American strategists; and more than one hundred Democratic Socialists of America members volunteered for her campaign, many of whom were white, and this proud Latina got plenty of love from her own community.

By the time she decided to run, the 14th District had become majority-minority and had given Bernie Sanders 41 percent of their vote in the last presidential primary. The political and demographic shift meant Ocasio-Cortez had a chance, despite campaigning against Joe Crowley, a powerful member and a rising star in the Democratic Party.

Remember, Joe Crowley believed that Trump was his prime adversary, but really it was the discontentment of people who were craving fundamental change and some kind of diversity in their representation. When they met the firebrand AOC, she could speak with them in English and Spanish, even if her Spanish was imperfect at times—something she's been open about and that has resonated with many

¡BORICUA!
ONE WAY
PUERTO
RICAN
PRIDE
ALEXANDRIA
¡OCASIO!
CORTEZ

younger Latinx Americans. She could salsa and would spend time in their homes after work. They knew she cared about the issues that were important to them, and she was there campaigning and trying to win them! Where was he? He was like that uncle who just sends a card with money on holidays because he's too "busy" to come by the house. Crowley probably wasn't a bad guy, he was just focused on a scope beyond his constituents. His district was changing yet he was remaining the same. He took his election for granted, spending too much time with the bigwigs in Washington and not enough with the people.

He had the means to win; he raised more than $2 million for his campaign. He was known for his ability to fundraise. AOC started with no real funds, but she was an activist and an organizer. She had only $300,000 in the bank from grassroots door-to-door campaigning; "no corporate backing" was her mantra. Endorsements came from organizations like MoveOn, Democracy for America, and the People for Bernie Sanders. She knocked on doors and sat down in people's homes. She talked to them about their lives, what was troubling them and what was troubling *her* about their struggle, you know. Beyond just connecting with her as a candidate who seemed more like them than Crowley was, they began to see her as an advocate who could stand up for them in Congress.

It also didn't hurt that AOC's campaign was fun and

creative! *What? Is that allowed in politics?* She organized happy hours in the community. There were photos of her speechwriting on the subway. There was even a documentary being filmed in part about her campaign, *Knock Down the House*, by Emmy-nominated director Rachel Lears. Not unlike AOC's campaign, the film was a scrappy, people-powered operation: Lears had started a Kickstarter campaign to fund it.

Those bold, uplifting campaign posters she had? They were donated in-kind from Tandem, a design firm dedicated to using persuasive marketing and advertisement "to advance the greater good." They have also designed signage for social-justice initiatives, organizations like Planned Parenthood advocating to protect *Roe v. Wade*. The image on Alexandria's campaign posters was obviously inspired by Obama's iconic "HOPE" posters.

And hope was a major part of what kept this little campaign going. Hustling all the way through, AOC knocked on doors and rallied volunteers, keeping the movement humming along, even when the media wasn't giving her a second thought.

And then there were the debates.

Crowley was called out for being a no-show. Odd, because debates were definitely part of campaigning and winning votes. *side-eye* But this guy was too comfortable. After missing two debates in the primary, he finally sent over a surrogate. Huh? And he *certainly* made sure that he sent over a

Latina in his place, because his opponent was Latina. *Isn't this what diversity looks like?* NO!

The event was hosted by *Parkchester Times*. Crowley said there were scheduling conflicts and he had to attend a civic meeting in Queens instead. That's why he sent over Annabel Palma, but *Parkchester Times* had no record of his desire to change the date. It was awkward at best. AOC tweeted that he'd sent, "a woman with a slight resemblance to me."

As portrayed in *Knock Down the House*, Alexandria Ocasio-Cortez didn't show up like she owned the place, ready to take down this guy Crowley. There was a little bit of imposter syndrome going on, sis. She's human. But she just kept showing up. And that's the cherry on the success sundae. The pep talk she gives herself in the documentary is a mantra all queens can adopt on the rise up—'cause Lord knows a queen needs an anthem. Going big ain't all rosé, girl, and AOC had to be her own bandleader. "I am experienced enough to do this," she tells herself. "I am mature enough to do this. I am brave enough to do this."

She knew that in the debates if Crowley went low—"This whole time, he's gonna tell me I can't do this. He's gonna tell me I'm small, I'm little, that I'm young, that I'm inexperienced." Well she was going to have to kung-fu block him with that Michelle Obama fire, and go high!

Then, whoa, don't be fooled by a queen's moment of weakness, honey, it was a brass-knuckled takedown after that. She was still only twenty-eight years old and basically unknown to him, but she was a *boss*, sorry he hadn't known it yet. 'Cause he'd know it once he faced her head-on.

In the debates, he got a taste of her power. She'd shut down his arguments, exploit his weaknesses, and in a live debate on NY1 you would have almost feared for Crowley, the way he was almost sweating and squirming in his seat while this woman tore his argument apart about the US Immigrations Control and Enforcement Agency (ICE) in a passionate rage (bold emphasis added, sis, to show where she smacked that set's table to underscore her point):

"You know what, if this organization [ICE] is as fascist as you've called it . . . **Then. why. don't.** you adopt the stance to eliminate it. **This. is. a. moral.** problem and your response has been to apply more paperwork to this situation. That puts our communities in danger, and it also conveys a profound misunderstanding of how we should be approaching this problem."

AOC was mad, not necessarily at Crowley himself, but at his politics. He was wasting his constituents' time while the nation was under attack by white nationalism, along with so many other issues. She was vocalizing what others felt. If Democrats like him were *about that life*, they needed to be more vocal about what was downright wrong! There was no time for games, or for shallow posturing. She put Crowley on the spot, and he was shut down because he wasn't ready to live it the way she was.

Her voice against injustice raised a moral dilemma for the Democratic Party that struck at the core of the party's incapacity to win on the big issues: the lack of acknowledgment that racism was still a major gear driving this country, even when Barack Obama had been in the White House. Democrats did not fight hard enough to protect their own, and with movements on the rise like Black Lives Matter, Me Too, and Time's Up, people were looking for champions to speak up even to their liberal brethren who weren't addressing their needs. Crowley had everything an incumbent could ask for to take up that role, but all the institutional power he held was no substitute for that kind of deep connection. Ocasio-Cortez came at him strong and firm. She wasn't afraid to have a stance, to *pull up*, and before he could blink, his campaign was cooked.

Less than two weeks later, in the Democratic primary on June 26, 2018, she beat him by fifteen points! The 14th District had so many Democrats (like, seven times more Democrats than Republicans) that winning the primary basically meant winning the seat. She beat him in that primary, and he pledged to support her in November, but he still appeared on the ballot as a third-party candidate under the progressive Working Families Party in the general election! It caused a bit of controversy at the time. *C'mon, man. You lost fair and square!*

That November, she went on to win the general election

against Republican candidate Anthony Pappas with a whopping 78 percent of the vote, and become the youngest woman ever elected to Congress.

WE ALL KNEW she'd win—you picked up this book knowing that, right? But just for fun, let's go back to that exhilarating summer night. Alexandria and her supporters had gathered at a bar in the Bronx to watch the results roll in. Alexandria Ocasio-Cortez's name appeared on the television, and then her name just kept popping up on the screen again and again and again. The crowd went wild with proud, loud millennial joy.

She won!

Her performance in *Knock Down the House* was Oscar-ready, like Sally Field's "You like me, you really like me!" Except AOC was so shocked that she couldn't really speak— "Oh my God, oh my God, oh my God" was all that could come out as she steadily held her chest surrounded by her tearful supporters. Eventually, she was able to soak it all in, and realized that a speech was needed: "This victory belongs to every grassroots organizer, every working parent, every mom, every member of the LGBTQ community, every single person is responsible for this . . . What we've seen is that working-class Americans want a clear champion, and there is nothing radical about moral clarity in 2018."

Beautiful, right?!

Meanwhile, "SHOCKING" was the unfortunate sentiment on the Hill from our president. Trump tweeted:

> Wow! Big Trump Hater Congressman Joe
> Crowley, who many expected was going to take
> Nancy Pelosi's place, just LOST his primary
> election. In other words, he's out! That is a big
> one that nobody saw happening. Perhaps he
> should have been nicer, and more respectful, to
> his President!

Ugh, man-babies! WHY MUST EVERYTHING BE ABOUT HIM?!

He couldn't even let AOC get her reggaeton on before he started tweeting. But her positivity couldn't be crushed so easily.

When she won the general election that fall, and officially became a congresswoman-elect, AOC used her time to make it a win for us all:

This is what is possible when everyday people come together in the collective realization that all our actions, no matter how small or how large, are powerful, worthwhile and capable of lasting change.

Words cannot express my gratitude to every organizer, every small-dollar donor, every working parent and Dreamer who helped make this movement happen. And that's exactly what this is—not a campaign or an Election Day but a movement, a larger movement for social, economic and racial justice in the United States of America.

When I started this campaign a year ago, I was working in a restaurant in downtown Manhattan, and it wasn't because . . . we didn't launch this campaign because I thought I was special or unique or better than anyone else. We launched this campaign because in the absence of anyone giving a clear voice on the moral issues of our time, then it is up to us to voice them.

We launched this campaign because no one was clearly and authentically talking about issues like the corrupting role of money in politics, about the disturbing human rights violations being committed by ICE, by the fact that we had no one giving voice to the idea and the notion that an entire generation is graduating with crippling loads of student loan debt, a ticking time bomb for our economy.

No one was talking about these issues, and when no one talks about them, we have the duty to stand up for what is right.

I think about oftentimes that incredible day on June 26 when despite no attention, despite no media fanfare, despite *the fact that no one wanted for us to get the word out on what was going on, we were able to organize everyday people, knocking on our neighbor's door and despite being out-spent $4 million—18 or 13 to 1—despite the fact that we were running against a tenth-term incumbent, despite the fact that it was our first time running for office, despite the fact that we didn't have the money, despite the fact that I'm working-class—despite all those things we won.*

An AOC Cookbook

AOC is the only congresswoman who can cook up a meal in a slow cooker, serve her staff, and still live-chat about politics on Insta. #MillennialsAreIncredible! Gurl, just because Alex became a member of Congress doesn't mean she got too fancy for the rest of us. Here's a short list of some of her favorite dishes, whether she's at home in New York or doing the damn thing down in Washington.

Black Bean Soup

The congresswoman likes soup! And soup is a dish for a revolution because it can feed a crowd of volunteers, and anything goes in that pot. She went live making black bean soup, and, probably for the first time ever, black bean soup went viral!

Pernil-Style Turkey on Thanksgiving

It's a Puerto Rican–style turkey where you make pork shoulder instead and add some sofrito sauce! Finger-licking yum. Oh, and you gotta have the rice and beans, also dubbed the Poor Man's Meal. She told *Bon Appétit*, "We were poor, so I was used to eating rice and beans every day." But this dish still slaps, even when you've made it big on the Hill.

Roasted Pig

Every year for her parents' anniversary, her dad would dig up a traditional Puerto Rican roasting pit in the backyard and spend hours turning a whole pig on a pit until the meat was smoked crisp on the outside, juicy-tender on the inside. Let's call it doggone good.

Instant Pot Mac 'n' Cheese

Who knew mac 'n' cheese could be made in an Instant Pot? I'll tell ya who, AOC! This is one of the congress-woman's favorite meals to make for her team. And she's the Insta Pot queen, and known for soliciting recipes. "All meals, cuisines, and dietary choices welcome. They just need to be GOOD, don't put me onto things with no flavor," she tweets.

Popcorn and Wine!

This is how she lives when her bae isn't home. *heart emoji* Get home soon, Riley!

★ ★ ★ ★ ★ ★ ★ ★ ★ ★ ★ ★ ★

LEADER

I *smoked* this
race . . . I didn't
edge anybody out.
I dominated and
I'm going to
own that.

—ALEXANDRIA OCASIO-CORTEZ,
INTERVIEW WITH *THE NEW YORKER*, 2018

THE YOUNGEST WOMAN IN AMERICAN HISTORY TO SERVE IN CONGRESS

I'm taking my own freedom,
putting it in my stroll.
—Jill Scott, "Golden"

AOC's primary win that June was a sign of what was to come. Her success was sending an important message that women of color were echoing all over the country. *We're coming!*

On January 3, 2019, Alexandria Ocasio-Cortez was sworn in to the most diverse Congress in history.

The future of politics would be different. It would be improved, guys.

Alexandria hadn't been the first woman or the first Latina to do this. Back in 1972, Elizabeth Holtzman, thirty-one years old, staged a successful primary challenge against eighty-four-year-old (and *fifty-year incumbent!*) Rep. Emanuel Celler and became the youngest woman ever elected to the House at

100% Latina

that time. As mentioned, the first Latina congresswoman, Nydia Velázquez, won her first race at thirty-eight years old.

Alexandria's achievement followed in their footsteps, and her swearing-in was joyous and emotional. Her mother, Blanca, held the Bible that swore her in. Speaker Nancy Pelosi stood by Blanca's side. In classic millennial style, Alexandria posted about it on Insta.

> *As I raised my hand for the oath, my mother held the holy book & looked into [Nancy Pelosi]'s eyes. Afterwards, the Speaker said to her "you must be so proud," and my mother began to cry.*

ON DATING LIKE A QUEEN, BY AOC

Oh when you walk by every night
Talking sweet and looking fine.
—Mariah Carey, "Fantasy"

R ep. Ocasio-Cortez has a boyfriend, gurl. Riley Roberts is his name, and they met while in school at Boston University. It was a Friday-afternoon event hosted by the dean that they had both attended in "true nerdy fashion," and there was a Spidey-sense connection between her economics major brain and her heart when Riley started quoting information about tax cuts in the 1950s. Sound familiar, single queens? AOC met her partner Riley—as they like to refer to each other in that woke millennial way—when she was preoccupied with her passion and not actively looking for a man. Plus, Alexandria is way too fly and busy to be out kissing frogs. It's great, too, that she hasn't conformed to any pressure to marry right away now that she's on the Hill. Riley is sweet, with a big cheesy smile, six feet tall and totally stands out so much it looks like he's photobombing the pics they post together. Mom likes Riley too. Blanca told the *Daily Mail*, "I love him. He is the most loving, supporting person I've seen. He helped her tremendously during the election."

She's right. He's all about that AOC sauce. If he's not smiling in complete awe of his gf, he just stays low-key, you know, he's an IT guy. He's the head of Homebinder.com and a consultant to tech start-ups—overall, it sounds like this guy likes to be helpful, which makes him a smart companion for a queen.

They have a French bulldog named Deco (oh my gosh, so cute!), who also doesn't seem to need the public eye to validate his cuteness, and doesn't particularly enjoy the subway commute, according to Instagram. The three are private and homebodies. So we won't dig too deep here—all we need to know is that Riley is a good guy who treats AOC like the queen she is.

THE HOUSE OF REPRESENTATIVES

Kill 'em with kindness
Go 'head, go 'head, go 'head now.
—Selena Gomez, "Kill 'Em with Kindness"

The day after her swearing-in, on January 4, 2019, a video of AOC dancing with her friends in a reinvention of the 1980s cult film *The Breakfast Club* went viral. *Whaaat?*, cried the conservatives. A policymaker is not supposed to dance, let alone make videos. By golly, bemoaned the right-wing commentator who posted the video on Twitter. Somehow they saw this as a scandal, though they managed to ignore a whole lot of actually ugly stuff happening on their side of the aisle (**cough, cough** like so much of what the president gets in to).

What did AOC do in response to what was supposed to be some misogynistic bulldoze of a woman in power? They wanted her to feel guilty; they wanted her to apologize. If it were a male congress member dancing, would it have set off so much rage? No, it would've been charming, even cute,

Queens Know How To Have Fun

show the human side, you know? The cards had to be played differently for women. But, AOC did none of what they probably wanted. Instead, she posted a new video the next day! Boom. *cue gangsta lean* The video was right outside of her office. Next to her name plaque, so they'd know she'd done it on official territory. She points right at the camera and she starts shimmying to "War" by Edwin Starr, "War, huh, yeah / What is it good for?" *bop*

The post:

> I hear the GOP thinks women dancing are scandalous

> Wait till they find out Congresswomen dance too! 🐦

When AOC launched her social-media campaign, she had fewer than three hundred Twitter followers, sis, and her Facebook livestreams got fewer likes than a Dunkin' dozen. Basically, she was pulling numbers a little worse than your grandma's Facebook account. But by primary day, AOC had a five-figure following of sixty thousand. By January 4, she had 20.7 million views and more than 160,000 retweets of that video, and had surpassed most House members in social-media followings, including Speaker Pelosi, who had one of the highest follower counts on the Hill. Not only had

Alexandria Ocasio-Cortez become a politician, she was a proven influencer. It was her supporters on social media who helped her gain confidence as a young Latina woman in Congress and assured her that she deserved a seat.

OH, WAIT, SPEAKING of Pelosi, let's backtrack. In November 2018, less than a month after Ocasio-Cortez was elected to Congress, she made a bold move. She left her new member orientation to join more than two hundred climate activists sitting in Minority Leader Nancy Pelosi's office; the sit-in was organized by the Sunrise Movement, an environmental organization.

The Sunrise group had started out at Spirit of Justice Park, which is located near the Cannon Building. There, they were also joined by Rep. Rashida Tlaib (more on her soon) and 150 other volunteers. They made their way to Pelosi's office to advocate for the likely new Speaker to start a new select committee for climate change, which they wanted to be called the Select Committee on a Green New Deal. The committee would push an agenda of 100 percent renewable energy, which they argued would also create more jobs.

Creating new House committees is sometimes part of the Speaker's job. The Democrats had taken over the House, but the 115th Congress, which had a Republican majority, had still not come to an end; the election for Speaker would take place when the 116th Congress began in January 2019. Back in 2007, Speaker Pelosi had created the Select Committee on Energy Independence and Global Warming—though they were able to convene hearings about key issues, the committee was shut down when the Democrats lost the House (and Pelosi lost the speakership) in 2010.

The Democrats had just taken back the majority in the House, so Pelosi was in a position where she was up for re-election as Speaker. And the new wave of congresswomen formed a diverse group, some of whom advocated as the future of Congress. But it's impossible to move into the future without squaring up with the past, and that included powerful leaders like Pelosi. The queens had to come to terms.

As AOC told *The Intercept*, "The way things are done, has not always been getting results. We have to try new methods."

And it really was time for new methods—we need results on climate change *now*. The UN's Intergovernmental Panel released a report the previous October that warned that some aspects of climate change would be irreversible in as little as twelve years. (That's the year 2030, for all the sisters counting along at home. Yikes!) Change needed to happen, and it needed to happen fast. AOC told the Sunrise group, "Should Leader Pelosi become the next Speaker of the House, we need to tell her that we've got her back in showing and pursuing the most progressive energy agenda that this country has ever seen."

Pause. What must be understood is this: When a new

queen arrives on the Hill, though there's space made for all, there's still ultimately a lioness initiation process as it were, before she can enter the chambers of acceptance. One expects to be questioned, whether one is the new queen or incumbent. So the Queens of the Resistance could handle that. It's just the public who needed to understand it. There was no doubt that Pelosi was the OG, a party leader who'd been in Congress (and seniority *rules* in the House) longer than the new congresswomen, who'd become known as part of the Squad (more on that later, sis), but AOC could carry her weight.

And she understood why her insurgent style was off-putting to those who had been on the Hill for a long time. She described it to *Vogue* like this: "I think we're scared of things we're not familiar with, that show power . . . If a space-ship landed in your backyard, it's like, 'What the [bleep] is that? Is it going to hurt me?'"

Meanwhile, the protesters were lining Pelosi's personal office and all along the hallway. One by one all 150 of them handed Pelosi's staff their letters about climate change. Protesters come by Pelosi's office all the time, and even get arrested, but a representative-elect participating was a surprise. By 11:30 A.M., fifty-one protesters were arrested by the Capitol police for protesting outside of the Cannon Building. By that time, Ocasio-Cortez had left, but she had made it clear that she was serious about her commitment to change, even when it means challenging the established order of things.

Most new members of Congress would wait until they were sworn in to challenge the woman who would in all likelihood become the most powerful member of the House, but Ocasio-Cortez was concerned about a livable future, and it seemed worth upsetting the apple cart. One of her first orders of business after she was sworn in was to release a Green New Deal resolution that called on Congress to develop a plan to address climate change. Some criticized the ambition of the plan. Surely it was too large to pass in a divided Congress? Or would be way too expensive and would add to the national debt. Her first legislative step was just a resolution, they sneered; it could never have the impact of a comprehensive bill, which represented significant action on the issue. But with this step, she was trying to gather initial support in the House to make her intentions clear. She was "elected as part of a movement, and she intends to govern as part of a movement," Corbin Trent, her spokesperson, commented.

"We need a Green New Deal and we need to get to 100 percent renewables because our lives depend on it," Ocasio-Cortez told reporters. "The IPCC themselves, they say we have ten years left and I—not just as an elected member, but as a twenty-nine-year-old woman—am thinking not just about what we are going to accomplish in the next two years but the America that we're going to live in in the next thirty years." *Yasss*, a statement that would stamp the vision of her politics.

★ ★ ★ ★ ★ ★ ★ ★ ★ ★ ★ ★ ★

RESISTANCE

Get used to me
slaying.

—AOC, ON TWITTER

GIVE IT UP FOR MY SISTERS

Started from the bottom, now the whole team's f**kin' here.
—Drake, "Started from the Bottom"

I t was a homie love that started with a phone call. Boston city councilwoman Ayanna Pressley was on an Amtrak train to New York in June 2018 when she asked her campaign manager to call up the congressional candidate Alexandria Ocasio-Cortez to ask her to stop by a fundraiser being held at her friend's apartment in Manhattan. As Pressley described it to *Business Insider*, as soon as AOC walked in there was an instant connection. "I was in the middle of my stump [speech] when Alex walked in. She's diminutive in size, but large in presence. She's luminous. I felt literally the air shift and I looked to my left and it was her entering the event space." They conversed in the living room.

"This is not just a blue wave, this is a movement that's

coming to Congress this year," said AOC to the small audience there.

"Absolutely. We called their bluff. When we had the Women's March, they thought it was just a moment. We knew we were ushering in a movement," said Pressley.

The living room was instantly on fire—a sisterhood had immediately taken effect.

AOC tweeted after the event. "Last night I had the honor of meeting @AyannaPressley and our BFF applications are already in."

They bonded over their shared experience studying at Boston University and working in a Kennedy's office. Pressley interned with Joe Kennedy II while in college, and AOC with Ted Kennedy. Pressley and AOC had both lost their fathers at a young age. AOC was excited that they were both running successful campaigns without any corporate money and "taking down political machines that don't service their communities."

Ayanna said, "You know how there are people who have Instagram relationships? This is not an Instagram relationship. Our relationship is not static, it is not one-dimensional, it is dynamic, it is deep, it is meaningful, it is real, and it grows day by day."

Ayanna Pressley became the first Black congresswoman from Massachusetts. Before she made history in her congressional election, Pressley was the first Black woman to be elected to the Boston City Council. A fellow sistren of progressive policy, she has spoken about sexual assault and adamantly argues on behalf of survivors and abortion rights. Like AOC she is bold in her legislation and one of her first amendments introduced to the House was to reduce the voting age from eighteen to sixteen.

Pressley, Ocasio-Cortez, and two other new, progressive members of Congress—Ilhan Omar of Minnesota and Rashida Tlaib of Michigan—have become known as the Squad. Omar and Tlaib are the first two Muslim women elected to Congress. The four women have proven to be ride-or-die BFFs through thick and thin.

Rep. Omar was born in Somalia. Her family fled a civil war and lived in a refugee camp in Kenya for years. She came to the United States as an asylum-seeker when she was ten and became a citizen at seventeen, and now she is a powerful force speaking truth to power in Congress. In another trailblazing moment, she became the first woman to wear a hijab on the House floor, ending the House's 181-year ban on headwear.

Rashida Tlaib is the first Palestinian-American woman in Congress and, along with AOC, one of the first two women from the Democratic Socialists of America (DSA) to serve as a Congress member. Soon after being sworn in, Tlaib famously said about Trump, "We're going to impeach the mother***er." (And do you know what? Less than a year later, the House did just that. Ha!)

Sis, let's be clear on what has been done to these women by Trump and his conservative loyalists. Fox News host Tucker Carlson claimed that Omar had once married her own brother; there have been absurd, unfounded questions about whether she's really an American citizen, the same jabs that Trump took at Obama. For some oddball, racist reason, conservative radio host Rush Limbaugh went on for weeks continuously and purposely overenunciating AOC's name, Alexandria Ocasio-Cortez, with a mock Spanish accent, elongating each syllable; Trump dismissed her last name "Ocasio-Cortez" as too difficult to pronounce; at a party for the Conservative Political Action Conference people scribbled the word "stupid" on a cardboard cutout of her face.

The women as a group have been called the Jihad Squad by conservatives. Trump's bogus remarks about how they should "go back to where they came from" if they don't like this country, caused the House Democrats to join together to condemn the president about what Pelosi said was a racist remark, but only four Republicans joined them; they even responded that Pelosi's comments, not the discriminatory name-calling, violated House rules.

In turn, Trump called the Squad racist, weak, and anti-American and "not very smart."

INSANE!

Yet, the Squad remain an inspiring force. They are four women who didn't enter politics as some token diversity girls, where they'd sit quietly and just serve face. Nope. Voters around the world wanted to have a rep who looked like and understood them and then the nation celebrated what they embody as well. In a CBS interview with Gayle King, Tlaib said, "We are an extension of a movement in our country that wants Medicare for All, that wants us to end mass incarceration, that wants us to push back on the attacks on communities of color."

Omar said, "We are a disruption to the business as usual that has been Washington."

Pressley said, "Each of us bring our unique and individual voice to this body. We govern in our own way. What we are are four women who have an alignment of values [and] shared policy priorities."

These women are America's response to all the mess that became the Trump election. Enough is enough.

They are fearless and outspoken in their criticism of the Trump administration, and progressives continue to cheer them on, even provide protection for them, such as when one hundred Black women hosted a rally in April 2019 to protect Omar against the attacks and threats on her life that she had been getting. Even Nancy Pelosi, used to facing threats on her life, had to order more Capitol Hill security for Omar.

The good news is that the Squad probably isn't going anywhere. They are incumbents now. They're going to continue to fight, to stick together in sisterhood, and no amount of bullying is going to stop them from resisting.

YO, NEW YORK IN THE HOUSE

I'm in control—never gonna stop.
Control—to get what I want.
—Janet Jackson, "Control"

S is, Alexandria Ocasio-Cortez's first few weeks in the 116th Congress were plenty eventful. There wasn't a dull moment when she shuttled off on her train commute from New York to DC. By January 4 she had cosponsored her first legislation, HR 242, opposing the PAYGO Act, a "pay as you go," budget-neutral rule where new programs that require spending by the House, either be paid by tax increases or budget cuts. What flows in must flow out, and the mantra had seemed to make sense after so many budgetary telenovelas, including the 2001 dot-com crisis that sent tax revenues flooding over and when a Republican-led House made it difficult for the Clinton administration to spend the windfall.

But now, along with other progressives, including Rep. Pramila Jayapal, who sponsored HR 242, AOC believed that PAYGO was also a way of handicapping their agenda, including their ability to mandate Medicare for All; PAYGO could make it a bipartisan issue that would be impossible to execute. Even though the bill had thirty-two cosponsors, including her friends in the Squad, ultimately the budget passed with PAYGO included. Still, her support for repealing PAYGO put her up against Pelosi and many others in the Democratic caucus—HR 242 wasn't brought up for a vote. But like all of the Queens of Resistance, AOC went into politics with the understanding that there are times when a queen's strength comes from her ability to break from the pack and stand on her own. As we chant, "Fight the power" Public Enemy–style, and praise AOC's courage, the truth is, it doesn't always come as easily as it looks, and on the Hill she almost daily must face the scrutiny of her colleagues. And PAYGO was one fight she didn't win.

But there would be more rules to follow and more to resist. And even though this first challenge didn't succeed, AOC's new colleagues were impressed. She was making a statement on the Hill—that she was coming in questioning everything and everybody, certain that age-old authority and rules would be unpacked, and she wasn't just going to be polite and follow the sheep if she believed it could hinder progress. Because she was there for progress, ya know!

JANUARY 4, 2019, was a busy day for our queen. On the same day as the PAYGO challenge, AOC was assigned to the House Oversight and Reform Committee, the main committee that regulates the administration and became the spearhead for impeachment, then chaired by the late, deeply respected Rep. Elijah Cummings. Several of the progressive new members were placed on the committee along with her, including Ayanna Pressley, Rashida Tlaib, and Katie Hill. Cummings liked these new young members. He admired their energy and intelligence, and wanted to put them under his wing. AOC was also put on the House Financial Services Committee, led by the first woman chair and fellow Queen of the Resistance Maxine Waters, who also signaled her willingness to mentor an up-and-coming firebrand. AOC also wanted to be placed on the powerful Ways and Means Committee, but she didn't get the nod.

Still, there were plenty of opportunities to make waves in the committees she was placed on. The House Oversight and Reform Committee is the investigative body of the House and would be the committee to open investigations on Trump and his administration. It also investigates other major issues Americans face, like skyrocketing healthcare costs, which was a major issue for our queen—more on that soon. Let's just say, it was on!

Still, the media and some of her new colleagues whispered about how this new Cardi-B-bopping freshman member (if they even knew who Cardi was) would conduct herself in congressional hearings. How prepared would she be? Would her lines of questioning be targeted enough? It was ridiculous talk.

Yet AOC is a queen because she keeps it 100. She would remain just as transparent as she had been during her campaign. With the country and her constituents watching, she shared her insecurities about the days ahead in her new job and what we're sure turned into sleepless nights about whether she'd screw it all up or not—common moments for anyone repositioning herself for a big new role. AOC doesn't want other women to think she's Superwoman. She wants more than anything for women to know they can and should do it too. She was honest about her learning curves and public about her insecurities as a new girl on the Hill. She didn't wait twenty years to write a political memoir; she knew that other women needed to know the real deal right away.

In fact, she let us know the details like no other. When she joined with the committees she shared the ins and outs of her new job in a Twitter thread and gave us the tea on Congress. "This week our 1st-ever Committee meetings and our 1st-ever Hearings of the 116th Congress (the oversight hearing was on the skyrocketing costs of prescription drugs). It's always intimidating to speak up in a new setting. In Congress, we abide by strict rules of communication, particularly in committee. For example you're supposed to address the chair, and speak in the third person when referring to your colleagues. Breaking those rules can have consequences small and large: not knowing how means you could lose precious speaking time, or miss an opportunity to make a point. Opposing party members are always looking for the slightest slip-up to gum up process or make an example of you."

Well, dang, that doesn't sound so fun. That sounds stressful! We knew already that AOC came in ready to advocate for her constituents and to encourage bold, progressive change . . . but first she did need to learn how the process works, just like all the other newbies.

But AOC says that she fights all of that noise by knowing how to communicate with her fear. Though the House environment is scary, she admits, she also saw it as a galvanizing force. As she says, "Fear, a lot like discomfort, forces us to choose: 'Do I do this, or not?'"

And thank goodness AOC and other queens are not afraid of some little roller-coaster moments, and neither should you be. If it's for the good, choose to do it.

By August 2019, she was already using her voice in a powerful way to discuss healthcare. "When I was sixteen years old, my father was diagnosed with a rare form of lung cancer," she said at a prescription-drug-prices hearing held by the House Oversight and Reform Committee. "He was in experimental trials in order to save his life. My family almost lost our home in order to try to keep him alive and just try to keep our family together." With that personal connection, she was bringing big issues in front of voters and getting people excited about change in policy issues that they may not have thought they could have any power in. She was living proof that they could, either by running for office themselves or by getting the right elected officials to fight for them.

It was the same energy she'd brought to her door-knocking days during the campaign, but now she was connecting with people via her story on a national scale. Healthcare issues were why AOC, a college-educated millennial, was working behind a bar when we met her. It wasn't because she just thought it would be fun to work behind a bar (not that anything is wrong with working behind a bar!). But something was wrong with the fact that she was working there because she'd had a loved one get sick and her family was thrown off course financially.

The United States is the only developed nation that doesn't guarantee universal healthcare. If AOC had lived in France or Ireland, her dad would have been cared for without that financial strain. If she'd lived in Demark, Italy, Austria, Germany, Japan, Costa Rica, Thailand, Brazil, Peru, and other places you vacation, he would have been covered. Medical bills are the number-one reason that Americans file for bankruptcy. Let me tell you something right now, sis: many Americans are paying their accumulated medical bills with credit cards, which then leads to a low credit score and converts into a years-long stumbling block for any future personal growth . . . and, oh, there's the fifty trillion phone calls coming from collection agencies. While people are trying to heal, the money stress itself is sickening.

Unfortunately, a risk of a health issue—from the minor to the major—can be catastrophic and life-altering in more ways than just physical health. People without insurance are the ones who pay the most for healthcare. They don't have insurance because they can't afford it or their employer doesn't provide support. These uninsured people are not just low-income service workers; the uninsured also include entrepreneurs, small-business owners, artists, and people whose employers keep them on only as contractors or part-time employees. A Harris Poll found that 54 percent of Americans delayed getting healthcare. "Making it" is a struggle, as we know, and it's more than an emotional burden when any sneeze or sniffle is a possible financial threat. Many people just decide to never acknowledge getting sick, period. *"Oh, Mami, it's just a cold that has been in my system for two months. No biggie."* The poorer she is, the less likely she is to be cared for. It's a decision whether to shuffle along, sick but free of medical debt, or to seek treatment and be exposed to another kind of risk.

"I was uninsured seven months ago," AOC said to the committee on the day of that hearing. "It's not just a financial issue. It is the stress . . . everything becomes a spiral [of] anxiety because you don't know how you're going to afford it . . . I rationed my own healthcare for ten years . . . We are rationing our own care." Right before she became congresswoman, AOC, while living in Parkchester in 2017, reported annual earnings of around $26,581. That means if she purchased health insurance, she would have had to pay approximately $160 per month. AOC once tweeted:

> Pretty sure one of Dante's Circles of Hell includes scrolling through a mirror-hall of agonizingly similar healthcare plans like "UHG Choice Master HMO 1800" vs "RedGo Option Plus EPO 2000." I don't know one normal person in this country that actually enjoys open enrollment.

At least if people could go to the doctor and feel financially "safe," there could be more preventative care. A blood test or even annual visits to the doctor for physicals and checkups could stop millions of us from acquiring serious illnesses. Instead, people are forced to delay their care. Instead, many people wait until they have to be hospitalized before treating their ailment. Emergency rooms are often full of people who are uninsured, either because they're unemployed or working hard at low-paying gigs or institutions that don't support their care. If they had health insurance, they could go to a regular doctor's office, but without it, the ER is their only viable option.

By law, hospitals must provide medical care to uninsured individuals. However, doctors are not required to offer care to uninsured people; so there won't be any follow-up care unless they have the Benjamins to pay out of pocket.

These inequalities, as with pretty much all systems of inequality, disproportionately affect people of color. Twenty-one percent of Hispanic people were uninsured in 2015, and 12 percent of Black people—only 8 percent of white people. Many Black and Latinx people *die* due to heart disease and diabetes at alarming rates—both preventable diseases if tackled early, deadly when untreated. Black people have the lowest life expectancy in the nation. The death rate of Black people was 1.2 times higher than white people in 2014. These are the dark, ugly consequences of our healthcare system that political warriors like AOC are fighting to abolish.

To combat this system, AOC is fighting for Medicare for All. Americans young and old are fed up with the sky-high bills and maze of networks—not to mention the knowledge that their hard-earned money is going into the pockets of insurance company CEOs. Medicare for All would mean the end of that for-profit system. Call it socialism, call it leftist thinking, or whatever, boo, AOC is fighting not for the name but for lives. She's experienced it, she had to clean toilets because of it, and now she's in public service to fix it.

But let's back up for a minute. Of course, President Barack Obama took a similar leap more than a decade ago with Obamacare, the nickname for the Patient Protection and Affordable Care Act (ACA for short). It offers access to healthcare and insurance to reduce healthcare spending in the United States through a number of regulations, taxes, tax breaks, mandates, and subsidies. A whole lot of issues have been addressed. There are now regulations where insurers can't deny insurance to sick people, or those with preexisting conditions. Before Obamacare, if you were, let's say, a breast-cancer survivor who lost your insurance, it was almost impossible to get new insurance. It was easier—and more profitable—for companies to insure a person in perfect health. This is what happens when profit drives the conversation about our health.

Other benefits that Obamacare brought included: subsidies, assistance from the government with out-of-pocket costs and health-insurance premiums; a mandate for everyone to be insured, an official order from the government for large employers to provide health insurance to their full-time employees; and taxes on those pharmaceutical and drug companies who profit off the sick. Young people were able to remain on their parents' insurance until they were twenty-six years old. Insurers couldn't deny coverage or care, or charge higher premiums to those with preexisting health issues. It expanded mental health and addiction coverage, including screenings for depression and behavioral assessments for children, at no cost. It isn't perfect, but it protected Americans.

But where is Obamacare now?

Well, there is what is known as Trumpcare, the healthcare reform of Obamacare under Donald Trump. He started his administration with an effort to repeal and reshape the original plan with a cheese-head's agenda. The GOP-controlled House and Senate came dangerously close to passing a plan that would have sent us way back to the bad old days when it came to healthcare, but thankfully the American people flooded their local town halls and slapped down that effort, *hard*.

Still, the Republican-led 115th Congress had been able to undermine the existing system: narrower networks and shorter enrollment periods, making it harder to participate in the program for people who need it; cuts to cost-sharing reduction assistance payments for insurers that provided help to those with lower incomes; changing coverage for birth control so religious employers don't have to cover contraceptives; and allowing individual states to implement work requirements for Medicaid.

A bogus, whackjob plan, just like its owner.

In the decade following its passage, the ACA allowed twenty million people to gain health insurance, and eleven million to obtain Medicaid in thirty-one states. Looking to the future, Alexandria the Great is going after Medicare for All to create a single-payer healthcare system. She tweets, "People don't want overly complicated choice[s] between pricey, low-quality plans. We want an affordable solution that covers our needs, like the rest of the modern world. Medicare for All:—Single-payer system—Covers physical, mental, & dental care—0 due *at point of service.*" Medicare for All allows for universal health coverage at a lower cost.

While she was once estimated to pay about $160 per month for insurance in 2017, today she and fellow Congress members can pay less than $80 a month and get to keep that insurance for life. It's a perk that ensures top-notch healthcare to those serving our country, but like her dad, AOC lives by the idea that if I eat, you eat too. "It's frustrating that Congress members would deny other people affordability that they themselves enjoy. Time for #MedicareForAll," she tweets.

Shoot, she needs pharma to step up their game too. AOC's from da Bronx and will fight so that all people have access to safe and affordable prescription medication. AOC pushed this agenda forward during the Congressional Oversight and Government Reform Committee investigation of the pharmaceutical corporation Gilead in May 2019.

Gilead produces an HIV-prevention drug known as Truvada for pre-exposure prophylaxis (PrEP) that is available globally. Taking it daily can drastically decrease the chances of contracting HIV-1 in people who are HIV negative, which is a game-changer, especially for the LGBTQ+ community. The problem is that the drug is prohibitively expensive for Americans, despite the fact that it was developed and patented in the United States. A quick comparison: Many in the United States need to pay more than $1,700 per month for Truvada, while it costs $8 per month in Australia, where it's available as a generic drug. *What?!* This is what happens when a government doesn't keep up with other developed nations on social programs like universal healthcare: everyday people are often unable to take a potentially life-saving drug, and the company gets to swim in cash like Scrooge McDuck. In 2018, Gilead made $3 billion in revenue globally.

AOC drilled the CEO of Gilead in the hearing. "This isn't about you as an individual or your character. This is about the system on incentives that you have set up. When it comes to who to blame for this, I don't blame you. I blame us. I blame this body, because every single developed country in the world guarantees healthcare as a right except us."

Now, thanks to the persistence and badass elected officials, including AOC, a generic version of Truvada will be available a year earlier than planned. This benefits individuals who can't afford the brand-name drug, but also everyone in the nation because the boost to public health created by accessible preventive care will save taxpayers billions.

A QUEEN SPEAKS up. AOC shows that it's time to be the loudest woman in the room about what we want to see. One should be able to go to the dentist without worrying about the rent, or student loans, or even her sneaker budget. Healthcare should be a given.

Many hardworking citizens would love a smile like AOC's, which gleams out at you in her official House photo and all over Instagram. The problem is the money stress associated with going to the dentist. One could go in for a regular cleaning, even with her employer insurance, and walk out with clean teeth and a $200 debt. *Shoot*, forget it if she was hyped about going to the out-of-network dentist that her co-worker recommended—that bill could skyrocket up without coverage.

And this is only one example. What about more serious diseases, ailments, or injuries that can't go untreated? AOC got into politics to fight with us and get us out of these holes. Some of us will be better at writing letters the old-fashioned way, others will go to town hall meetings to speak with elected officials in person, and others will take to social media with a fierce finger or live video from their phones. But whatever the method, AOC helped this generation understand that whatever you do, you be sure to clap back.

---⭐---

CLAP BACK

I don't see nobody else
'Scuse me while I feel myself.
—Lizzo, "'Scuse Me While I Feel Myself"

I n Alexandria Ocasio-Cortez's first days in office, in addition to being tweeted at and saluted by another queen, music legend Cher, for her abilities as a congresswoman to mix dance moves, a great lipstick shade (Beso by Stila), and cosponsoring a bill, AOC was also going blow for blow with Congress members on the other side of the aisle. And these weren't cute little jabs. She said straight-up what many people all over the world were thinking when she called the president out as "a racist" in an interview on *60 Minutes*. While the haters tried to dub her a "flamethrower," or however you describe a queen who can light up a movement, AOC remixed it into a compliment and told Anderson Cooper on CNN, "I like to think that I'm persuasive, and so I think a lot of that work is going to be on building relationships and trying to persuade and talk to my colleagues on building a progressive agenda for the party."

That seems like a pretty positive agenda, right? But the haters keep trying her, and they have been since her big primary win made her a national figure. Back in December 2018, not long before she was sworn in, she had to clap back at the president's son Donald Jr. after he went online and claimed her tax proposals and "socialist ideology" would lead "Americans to having to eat their dog's food." He was fearmongering about her proposal for a 70 percent marginal tax rate that would apply only to a person's income *above $10 million*, not for their entire income.

The next day she shot back,

> I have noticed that Junior here has a habit of posting nonsense about me whenever the Mueller investigation heats up.
>
> Please, keep it coming Jr—it's definitely a 'very, very large brain' idea to troll a member of a body that will have subpoena power in a month.

On January 15, she had to school another figure on the right, former Wisconsin governor Scott Walker, about marginal tax rates.

> @ScottWalker: Imagine if you did chores for
> your grandma and she gave you $10. When you
> got home, your parents took $7 from you. The
> students said: 'That's not fair!' Even 5th graders
> get it.

Ocasio-Cortez countered:

> @AOC: Explaining marginal tax rates to a
> far-right former Governor: Imagine if you did
> chores for abuela & she gave you $10. When
> you got home, you got to keep it because it's
> only $10 . . . Then we taxed the billionaire in
> town because he's making tons of money
> underpaying the townspeople

AOC was being attacked, but she could clap back with the best of them, and it only made Americans love her more. True to form, she told Cooper exactly how she felt about the haters. Did she feel guilty or bad about these Twitter spats? No. "If you can't take the heat, then get out of the kitchen. And people know that if you're going to come after me, you're opening yourself up." Don't come to rumble with AOC, #SheReady.

That's not to say some of the haters didn't get pretty scary.

By May 2019 she was getting death threats just for being who she is, sis. "I've had mornings where I wake up and the first thing I do with my coffee is review photos of the men (it's always men) who want to kill me," she explained. "I don't even get to see all of them. Just the ones that have been flagged as particularly troubling. . . . It happens whenever Fox News gets particularly aggressive plus hateful too." Fox News has been *soooo* angry, *soooo* vampire thirsty for the young congresswoman's blood that they continue to try to suck all the life out of her reputation as a Queen of the Resistance.

According to a study done by Media Matters (April 2019), she was mentioned 3,181 times within six weeks on Fox News Channel and Fox Business Network, from February 25 to April 7—just under seventy-six times a day. In a five-minute span on a single night, Fox News host Tucker Carlson called her "stupid," "a bigot," and described her platform as "pure poison and open racism." He described her developing influence in Congress in the following terms: "over time like any untreated virus, her bigotry grew more inflamed." And those are the softer blows, Tucker has also called her an "idiot windbag," "pompous little twit," and a "fake revolutionary," according to *USA Today*. Fox commentator Brit Hume said, "She's kind of adorable in a way that a five-year-old can be adorable," taking jabs at her age.

Basically, Fox News will twist and try to destroy everything she says—including both blatant and suggestive remarks about pictures of her with other Congress members, like Pelosi, to paint her as disrespectful and to stir up a frivolous debate. Sean Hannity once said, "She's the real Speaker of the House" as if he's trying to drive a wedge between AOC and Speaker Pelosi. Thank goodness Pelosi's a queen who can see right through that BS. But like some sort of burly Bluto, Fox continues to attempt to bully AOC about her liberal values to recruit drama for her on her own side, stirring up stories that paint her as being anti-Democratic establishment and a communist.

They just loved her tussle with Whoopi Goldberg on *The View* about how Whoopi felt left out of AOC's talk about the younger generation versus the old—they slice and dice and dub that scene as if Whoopi left angry. Note: She didn't. But that's what Fox News wants people to think.

They'll showcase wild meme-like photos of AOC during their segments with exaggerated expressions, nothing like her truly pleasant face, to portray her as a crazy-eyed lunatic or madwoman. A lot of the name-calling is blatant, and some of it is couched in strange compliments like when a "concerned" Laura Ingraham wondered whether Ocasio-Cortez would have to go to jail after an alleged campaign-finance violation . . . Oh but she also admires her political career. *Ewww, nice-nasty.* Shade! And somehow it's good for their ratings to stalk one of the youngest Congress members? But like AOC herself says, "We don't flinch," y'all.

DESPITE ALL THIS, she continued to slay on Capitol Hill too. On January 16, 2019, she made her first floor speech. To set the scene: The government was shut down because Trump was insisting that lawmakers agree to give him $5 billion to build his ridiculous border wall. This man was holding wages hostage for hundreds of thousands of government workers for this pet project of his! Ugh. At the hearing, AOC told the story of one of her constituents, a man from Yemen, an air-traffic controller who was struggling financially due to the government shutdown, all because Trump's tantrum was keeping the federal budget from being passed. She was driving home the point that the government shutdown was affecting regular citizens. The government was shut down for five weeks, there were major airline delays on the East Coast, and federal workers were missing their paychecks.

Rep. Ocasio-Cortez said on the floor, "The truth of this shutdown is that it's actually not about a wall . . . The truth is, this shutdown is about the erosion of American democracy and the subversion of our most basic governmental norms. It is not normal to hold 800,000 workers' paychecks hostage. It is not normal to shut down the government when we don't get what we want . . . It is certainly not normal to starve the people we serve, for a [wall] that is wildly unpopular with the American people."

True to form, AOC tweeted about the experience. "It was an honor to bring forward one of my constituents' stories in my first-ever speech on the House floor. In the moment, it often seems lonely and scary to speak out on these issues—especially in DC, which so deeply prizes conformity, 'etiquette' in the form of learned silence, and falling in line. I feel a lot of pressure to conform, or not shine as brightly—and I also admit that a lot of that pressure is self-imposed. In DC it 'feels' as though I shouldn't say or do these things more so than other contexts, because those feelings are reinforced by a culture that is very exact in who should be where on a totem pole."

AOC's speech would go viral and become one of CSPAN's most viewed videos. Look at that type of outreach. So many people got to hear her constituents' stories.

A FEW WEEKS later, at the State of the Union address, Alexandria Ocasio-Cortez appeared like a superhero in a white cape jacket. The female lawmakers wore white, as encouraged by the Democratic Women's Working Group to celebrate the record number of women elected to Congress and to pay homage to the women's suffrage movement. It was fitting for this president.

She had made a statement of her own that was already flying across media outlets: she arrived with Ana Maria Archila, a codirector of the Center for Popular Democracy. Archila worked with Make the Road New York and was dedicated to helping immigrant and working-class New Yorkers—and she lived in AOC's congressional district. Just a few months earlier, Archila and a fellow sexual assault survivor named Maria Gallagher had confronted Arizona senator Jeff Flake in a Senate elevator during the confirmation hearings of Supreme Court nominee Brett Kavanaugh, who stood accused of sexual assault. They confronted Flake, hoping to convince him to follow his conscience and vote against confirming Kavanaugh's nomination to the Supreme Court instead of voting along party lines. At the State of the Union, they wore matching pins that AOC had purchased at a local store in their district. One of them read WELL-BEHAVED WOMEN RARELY MAKE HISTORY. *snap, snap*

AOC's Resistance Skincare

FOR AVOIDING STRESS AND PIMPLES

You may have noticed that somehow Congress hasn't aged AOC yet. Here are some tips that could keep you looking as dewy and youthful as the youngest woman on the Hill! And this is how you take on a "witch hunt" without looking like a witch:

★ First: Ask yourself, "Do I have the power to change things or do I just have to ride it out?"

★ Avoid full coverage.

★ Cut back on dairy products.

★ Stick with the staples: tinted moisturizers, BB cream, mascara, blush, stick highlighter, brow gel, lip color.

★ Save the expensive stuff for fancy outings.

★ Toner should not have alcohol.

- ★ Don't be afraid of drugstore makeup.

- ★ Incorporate double cleansing if you wear a lot of makeup.

- ★ Do a facial mask every once in a while.

- ★ Use sunscreen.

- ★ Let your skin breathe if you're putting on makeup every day. As soon as you get home, remove your makeup so that your skin can breathe before you go to sleep.

- ★ Last but not least, slay.

★ ★ ★ ★ ★ ★ ★ ★ ★ ★ ★ ★ ★

QUEEN

Well-behaved women rarely make history.

—AOC'S ENAMEL PIN AT THE
2019 STATE OF THE UNION

RADICAL JUSTICE

Girls, we run this mutha.
—Beyoncé, "Run the World (Girls)"

When Alexandria Ocasio-Cortez spoke at the Women's March in Washington on January 19, 2019, she chose to define justice.

Justice is not a concept that we [just] read about in a book. Justice is about the water we drink. Justice is about the air we breathe. Justice is about how easy it is to vote. Justice is about how much ladies get paid. Justice is about whether we can stay with our children for a just amount of time after we have them—mothers, fathers, and all parents. Justice is about making sure that being polite is not the same thing as being quiet. In fact, the most righteous thing you can do is shake the table.

Last year we took power to the polls, and this year we're taking power to the policy. Let us remember that a fight means no person left behind. So when people want to stop talking about the issues that Black women face, when people want to stop talking about the issues that trans women or immigrant women face, we gotta ask them why does that make you so uncomfortable? Because now this is the time when we're going to address poverty. This is the time we're going to address Flint. This is the time we're going to talk about Baltimore and the Bronx and the wildfires and Puerto Rico. Because this is not just about identity, this is about justice. And this is about the America that we are going to bring into this world.

ONE OF THE principles of justice that Ocasio-Cortez went into Congress raising the alarm about was human existence, period. What grander scale is there than the future of Earth itself? That's why one of her central initiatives has been the Green New Deal.

In 2019, 12.5 billion tons of ice was reportedly melted. It was a sad time for ski bums. Sea levels are rising, producing some severe storms and deadly winds, increasing wildfires, droughts, and other extreme weather. There was a deadly mudslide in California; more than a half inch of rain fell in five minutes. The mud flattened homes and covered freeways. Streets in Maryland became raging rivers in a drastic storm where more than eight inches of rain fell in a few hours. The same with North and South Carolina, Florida, and Georgia, where Hurricane Michael was the worst storm since 1969. One hundred and fifty thousand acres and more than thirteen thousand homes were lost in the Golden State due to the devastating Camp Fire disaster.

This is all the result of climate change. The world is too hot and getting hotter. Scientists predict that there will be at least twice as many wildfires by 2050 as there were in 2019. Warming beyond 2 degrees Celsius will expose 350,000,000 people globally to deadly heat stress by 2050. It will cost money: $500,000,000,000 in lost annual output, damage to those beautiful waterside oases we love, with $1,000,000,000,000 of damage to public infrastructure and coastal real estate, and more. And it will take us to the grave quicker. Human life expectancy will decline due to the scarcity of basic needs of clean water and air, and healthy foods.

It's not only the wildlife suffering; people are being killed. In 2018 there were 315 natural disasters and 11,804 deaths, but more than 68 million people were affected. The economic loss was in the millions, taxpayers. According to AOC, the government must invest in dealing with these issues and make human existence a priority, rather than siding with big oil companies and climate deniers. Her Green New

Deal is an aggressive and economically focused policy to jump-start greater investments in clean-energy jobs and infrastructure. The benefits of AOC's proposal are twofold: (1) it will move the country to 100 percent clean energy in ten years (2) it will stimulate the creation of green jobs and introduce a new kind of economy, independent from reliance on fossil fuels.

The Green New Deal may be some straight-*fire* policy, no pun intended, but what most Americans want to know is, what the hell is it? Here are some of the Green New Deal's goals unplugged and decoded in layman's terms:

(A) to achieve net-zero greenhouse gas emissions through a fair and just transition for all communities and workers;

Unplugged translation: You can drive, and we can also still breathe easy.

(B) to create millions of good, high-wage jobs and ensure prosperity and economic security for all people of the United States;

Unplugged translation: Will allow another opportunity for your cousin to get off his parents' couch and get a good job saving the planet.

(C) to invest in the infrastructure and industry of the United States to sustainably meet the challenges of the 21st century;

Unplugged translation: To keep the country from falling apart (literally!) and not pollute the planet.

(D) to secure for all people of the United States for generations to come—(i) clean air and water; (ii) climate and community resiliency; (iii) healthy food; (iv) access to nature; and (v) a sustainable environment;

Unplugged translation: A healthy survival rate.

(E) to promote justice and equity by stopping current, preventing future, and repairing historic oppression of indigenous peoples, communities of color, migrant communities, deindustrialized communities, depopulated rural communities, the poor, low-income workers, women, the elderly, the unhoused, people with disabilities, and youth (referred to in this resolution as "frontline and vulnerable communities");

Unplugged translation: This one kind of speaks for itself.

Climate change is getting more intense as time goes on, and AOC understands the urgency of the issue. "I don't think that we can compromise on transitioning to 100 percent renewable energy. We cannot compromise on saving our planet. We can't compromise on saving kids," she says. "We have to do these things. If we want to do them in different ways, that's fine. But we can't not do them."

Climate change is accelerating, and the more storms we experience today will only increase what we see tomorrow. AOC is a millennial, and it's key that she is leading the charge on this. Her generation and beyond have to live on this planet for many years to come, and if the White House keeps burying its head in the sand on climate change, there could be even more damaging effects on her cohort personally.

Through the Paris Climate Agreement in 2016, member nations had committed to try to do what was necessary to restrict the global temperature increase to below 2 degrees Celsius by 2030—increases beyond that would be exponentially more catastrophic to the environment. (It's also definitely worth noting that the United States joined the Paris accords under Obama and then Trump pulled the country out of the agreement.)

This report described what would be required to limit global climate rise. Radical change is necessary—cutting coal consumption by one-third, ramping up new technologies that can remove carbon dioxide from the air, a necessary step toward reducing greenhouse-gas emissions. The report indicated that nations had only twelve years to take these steps, otherwise we will have run out of time to make the improvements that were necessary. We had already moved way beyond using easy options to make the change. The report also indicated that every little bit of progress made an impact. No change was too small to contribute to the reduced emissions that were necessary, and if we slammed on the brakes now, we might be able to halt some of the worst outcomes by 2050.

Young people, like seventeen-year-old Swedish climate activist Greta Thunberg, take these reports especially personally because it is their future that is being restricted and compromised. The issue was not lost on Alexandria, a woman with a star named after her. She sees climate change as an existential threat to all human and natural life, as well as an issue of equal justice.

Something had to be done, and Alexandria Ocasio-Cortez wanted to be a leader of the charge.

The name "Green New Deal" was not coined by Rep. Ocasio-Cortez though. It had been percolating around the fringes of the mainstream for some time. The term was actually coined by the journalist Thomas Friedman, who at the beginning of the mortgage crisis in 2007 was calling for taxes on carbon emissions, the end of fossil fuel subsidies, and incentives to promote wind- and solar-powered energy. Then candidate Barack Obama added a Green New Deal to his presidential platform in 2008, and in 2009 the United Nations

developed a Global Green New Deal, advocating government stimulus for the development of renewable energy technologies. Democrats made a stab at capping carbon emissions in the House, but the bill died in the Senate in 2010. Then the Labour Party in the UK, its democratic socialist political party, established a green investment bank, which was mightily opposed by the Conservative Party and also died.

Her backing of the GND made AOC an enemy of the status quo, in particular the big oil companies' status quo, and they've fought her at every turn. But it's a worthwhile fight, and we know by now that this queen will fight for us no matter how powerful the adversary may be.

★

FOR THE DREAMERS

I never really knew that she could dance like this
She makes a man want to speak Spanish.
—Shakira, "Hips Don't Lie"

While in college, one of the internships that AOC landed, and one that probably helped this queen put a firm stamp on switching majors from biology to economics was in Sen. Ted Kennedy's office. Often she'd be the only Latina in the room. It was in this context where she really discovered how damaging it is that women who looked like her were underrepresented in spaces like politics. That needed to be repaired if the proper care was going to uplift certain communities. "I was the only Spanish speaker, and [as a nineteen-, twenty-year-old] kid, whenever a frantic call would come into the office because someone [was] looking for their husband because they have been snatched off the street by ICE, I was the one that had to pick up that phone. I was the one that had to help that person navigate that system."

Growing up with a mom from Puerto Rico who spoke English as a second language, watching Blanca move in the world, seeing the disparity between Yorktown and the Bronx, she understood the needs of immigrant and communities of color beyond the splashes on the *New York Post* and other media. Beyond what Trump said about them. She knew firsthand that many of the people in these communities were working hard and fighting for a place in this country more than anything.

Her work in Kennedy's office had led her to communicate with people on a daily basis with similar stories of displacement and lack of support because of their status. These are people who believed in the promise of America.

Of course, this experience would eventually shape her own staffing choices and inform her politics for years to come. She hit the ground running on issues surrounding race and immigration basically as soon as she took office.

In June 2019, as the representative of the 14th District, Alexandria Ocasio-Cortez worked to support the passage of the American Dream and Promise Act. The bill directs the Department of Homeland Security to grant lawful permanent resident status to undocumented people who were brought to the United States as children younger than eighteen years old on the initial date of entry, also known as Dreamers. It would grant resident status for ten years and streamline procedures for permanent residence for immigrants who have completed programs in educational institutions or served in Uniformed Services.

That same summer, Trump's policies resulted in ICE basically showing up in ski masks to terrorize immigrant communities. Undocumented immigrants, especially those who'd crossed the border from Mexico, were their targets. It was just one part of an array of cruel measures from a president who had built a campaign around hate and bigotry. But his biggest problem at this time was his desire to build a wall along the Mexican border, keeping migrants and asylum-seekers out of a country that many of his followers thought should be whites-only. *Ooohh*, how he despised those people crossing the border. His visceral hate and disrespect toward Mexican people in particular was established from day one of his candidacy, and it was the evil fairy dust along his campaign trail. He promised to deport two million people when he took office. During his campaign speeches, Trump made a link between Mexican people to undocumented immigrants to criminals, and there was no separation—it was all one three-digit math equation and probably as far as he could think to take it. On the very first day of his campaign, he was popping off about immigration: "When Mexico sends its people, they're not sending the best. They're not sending you, they're sending people that have lots of problems and they're bringing those problems. They're bringing drugs, they're bringing crime. They're rapists and some, I assume, are good people, but I speak to border guards and they're telling us what we're getting." *Ugh*.

Not only are the president's ongoing comments like this blatantly racist, they aren't even close to accurate by the numbers. Mexican migrants make up only about half of all undocumented people living in the United States. Their numbers have decreased from 6.4 million in 2009 to 5.6 million in 2016. Further, fewer than 10 percent of undocumented immigrants living in the United States for less than five years are from Mexico. Maybe he's mixing up his Spanglish, because he's obviously misinformed about Mexico.

But what Trump was advocating for wasn't about numbers, it was white supremacy and the beliefs of the longtime bigots in this country who thought he was going to be their white savior. That's why he sent the country spiraling for five weeks in 2019 with a government shutdown trying to get the money for a dang wall.

It's also the founding ideology behind the 220-word description of Trump's foreign policy he posted on his first day in office. His inaugural speech had a bizarrely negative tone (phrases like "American carnage" came up during what was ostensibly a victory speech) and focused on "America first" concepts. He pardoned Sheriff Joe Arpaio of Maricopa County, Arizona, notorious for his misconduct against communities of color, that he was named in a class-action lawsuit for targeting Latino drivers and passengers. In fact, he faced 2,700 lawsuits concerning the county's prison violations, which is probably unsurprising given that he referred to his own prison as a "concentration camp." A few months after Trump pardoned him, Arpaio announced his intention to run for the Senate in 2018 (thankfully, he didn't make it out of the primary!).

Trump also signed an executive order to have ICE fulfill immigration law enforcement and funded an additional ten thousand ICE agents. The president of Mexico, aghast, had to establish defense centers with fifty consulates to protect people. Private prisons were used to house 65 percent of detained immigrants. They were detained for approximately fifty-two days if caught, and the Department of Homeland Security spent $126 per day for each detainee. Private for-profit prisons were making *dough*. The media showed America how kids were separated from their parents, *literally* taken away right before their eyes. It was horrifying, a permanent stain on our democracy.

In July 2019, Rep. Ocasio-Cortez marched down to these detention centers, along with other Congress members. *Real talk*, after her visit, AOC declared ICE a rogue agency. Along with other Americans, she was mad as hell about what she saw. It was disgusting policy, and she described the abhorrent violation of human rights that accompanied it: "Now I've seen the inside of these facilities. It's not just the kids. It's everyone. People drinking out of toilets." She left the detention centers disturbed, and she wasn't the only one. Other members of Congress said the same. There were cryptic details shared with the public by inspectors and media. In one location, only four showers were allotted for 756 people. A cell with a 55-person maximum capacity held 135 men, with only one toilet and one sink. Half the immigrants were held standing outside because there was no room inside; those kept inside were being held in cells at five times their maximum capacity.

One female inmate described the conditions to Rep. Ocasio-Cortez as "psychological warfare." She described how she and other women were woken up at odd hours and called whores by the officers. Congressman Joaquin Castro showed video footage on social media of his visit to El Paso Border Station #1, where women were on floors in large blue sleeping bags. He shared how they hadn't been able to shower for fifteen days and how they didn't have access to the medications they needed. Some were in emotional distress from being separated from their children.

Congresswoman Ocasio-Cortez is outspoken about wanting ICE completely eliminated. And as part of that, she was totally against any measures that would give the agency more power or money. This included a gun-control amendment to the 2019 budget that required gun sellers to notify ICE if an undocumented person tries to purchase a gun.

"ICE was created in 2003 along with the Patriot Act. It was a weapon waiting for a tyrant. I was upset that 26 Dems forced the other 200+ to vote for a pro-ICE provision at the last min without warning. Because I think an agency that pins children down + forcibly injects them w/ antipsychotic drugs shouldn't be given more power," AOC tweeted. "If you're mad that I think people SHOULD KNOW when Dems vote to expand ICE powers, then be mad. ICE is a dangerous agency with 0 accountability, widespread reporting of rape, abuse of power, + children dying in DHS custody. Having a D next to your name doesn't make that right." According to AOC, many Democrats were against the establishment of ICE since its beginning, post-9/11 when there was a strong push for more authoritarian legislation.

When the media showed AOC walking away from a facility, homegirl looked bent out of shape. Her discomfort in witnessing the treatment of the detainees firsthand was written all over her face. "I was not safe from the officers," is all she said to CNN. Other Congress members described the officers as "unwelcoming and uncooperative," and they also shared the blatant animosity they felt from the officers toward them.

IN JUNE 2019, the acting director of ICE, Mark Morgan, appeared on Hill TV. Many Americans were holding their hearts, devastated at what was happening to the migrant children, then he appeared with a personal demeanor resembling a black hole and dramatic sound bites that could have been written into *A Few Good Men*. "I feel very satisfied that if you go to these facilities, whether it's a border-patrol facility or [Health and Human Services] facility or an ICE facility that there will be safe and adequate conditions to detain individuals."

AOC obviously disagreed. "The fact that concentration camps are now an institutionalized practice in the 'Home of the Free' is extraordinarily disturbing, and we need to do something about it," she said on Instagram.

The GOP came down on Ocasio-Cortez for her use of the phrase "concentration camps" and exploited that to change the conversation. They steered the narrative away from what AOC and other Congress members had witnessed with their own eyes and ears when speaking to the people being held. Oh, *puhlease*. In true AOC fashion, she swung back: "For the shrieking Republicans who don't know the difference: concentration camps are not the same as death camps. Concentration camps are considered by experts as 'the mass detention of civilians without trial.' And that's exactly what this administration is doing."

Meanwhile, Donald Trump tweeted about the issue as if he were an employee at Terminix, "Next week, ICE will begin the process of removing millions of illegal aliens who have illicitly found their way into the United States. They will be removed as fast as they come in." How is *that* not more upsetting than someone using strong language to condemn appalling conditions?

AOC also had to throw down with former ICE acting director Larry Homan, who was appointed by Trump and served from 2017 to 2018, when he had a meltdown about the criticism coming from AOC and other Congress members.

At a congressional hearing on July 12, 2019, AOC tried to speak slowly and calmly so this guy could hear and understand the issues through his own prejudice that had allowed the organization to operate with such ill will. "Zero tolerance was interpreted as the policy that separated children from their [families]," she said.

His response: "If I get arrested for a DUI and I have a young child in the car, I'm gonna be separated [from my child]. When I was a police officer in New York and I arrested a father for domestic violence, I separated that father from—"

Eye-roll *Ahhhhhhh, how is this the same?*

AOC lowered her voice even further, though it's apparent she'd have liked to jump out of her leather seat across the room and shake him down. Instead she chose her words carefully, to educate this man about his job. "Mr. Homan, with all due respect, legal asylees are not charged with any crime."

She presented Homan with a memo he had signed back in April 2018 providing the recommendation to then Homeland Security secretary Kirstjen Nielsen recommending that the United States pursue family separation and zero tolerance at the border.

"I gave Secretary Nielsen numerous recommendations on how to secure the border and save lives."

AOC went in closer. "But it says here that you gave her numerous options but the recommendation was option three, family separation."

ICE's Homeland Security investigations are supposed to investigate criminal organizations that are a national threat, which includes immigration and financial crime, contraband and human smuggling, weapons, and so on—but it sure looked like most of the people caught up in this nightmarish policy were families just looking for a safe place to live.

At another hearing in September 2019, Homan hailed ICE as a bunch of do-gooders. *Riiiight*. He seemed to go on and on about how hurt he was about the way ICE was being portrayed—until finally, *pop*, AOC threw down; she'd had enough of this Mr. Homan dude, and ICE as a whole should get the message: *Your time is expired*. As she put it:

> *No child should ever be separated from their parents. No child should ever be taken from their family. No women should ever be locked up in a pen when they have done no*

harm to another human being; they should be given water, they should be given basic access to human rights. And it is a false notion: the idea that we have to choose between people is a false notion. No child should ever have to suffer for the benefits of another. And I will never accept that argument. Thank you.

AOC knew the effects of Donald Trump's ICE raids on the community from her days working in Flats Fix. According to the Pew Research Center, one-third of people working in the food industry are undocumented. These are the people whom AOC worked with and called her friends, and have been a target for ICE raids since 2003. But under the Trump administration ICE arrests skyrocketed by 37.6 percent, 41,318 arrests and climbed rapidly the further he got into his presidency and as AOC entered office. Flats Fix's kitchen was not raided, but she remembers the fear of it always hanging like smoke on the ceiling.

AS A CONGRESSWOMAN, she's focused on correcting criminal justice and immigration policies across the board. "My district contains Rikers Island," she said. "I cannot talk about the economic rights of families until those families are reunited by the separation of both our criminal-justice and immigration system. There's this false notion that you have to separate and choose between issues of class and issues of race. What people do when they say that you need to separate class from race is that they are really just saying that people of color should come second. There is no such thing as talking about class without there being implications of the racial history of the United States. You just can't do it."

To help protect these racially profiled communities, AOC cosponsored the Fair Chance Act, HR 1076, to prohibit federal agencies and contractors from requesting that applicants disclose their criminal history before they are given a conditional offer of employment. She's also active in working with politicians and organizers to end for-profit prisons and mass incarceration and end the school-to-prison pipeline; to release those incarcerated for nonviolent drug offenses; to end cash bails, which often keeps small offenders in prison longer than necessary; and to allow for independent investigations for individuals killed by law enforcement.

She also understands that these issues are all interconnected, and has adopted a policy approach that will help level the playing field nationwide. She has helped to pass HR 8, a bipartisan bill to establish new background-check requirements for firearms transfers between private parties, and supports gun reform and a federal ban on assault weapons, high-capacity magazines, and bump stocks.

To empower working-class communities, she works diligently toward equality and believes the heart of that matter to be high-quality education for all. Therefore she supported the Student Debt Cancellation Act of 2019, which advocates for loan forgiveness, and HR 3457 to amend the Higher Education Act of 1965 to ensure college for all.

AOC says, "There are a lot of people in this country who are counted out of everything. They're counted out of being seen as qualified; they are counted out in all sorts of ways and manners. I was counted out. When people who are counted out come together, that's power."

Women like Alexandria Ocasio-Cortez in the 116th Congress are counting them in.

"TOO LOUD? DO IT ANYWAY"

Never did I switch, story stayed the same
I did this on my own, I made this a lane.
—Cardi B, feat. Chance the Rapper, "Best Life"

One of the many lines of criticism that Republicans and her Democratic brethren alike use to condemn AOC is her appeal to democratic socialism. Alexandria describes her movement toward democratic socialism as organic. "It was a lot more about action than about descriptions or -isms," she said. She noticed that anytime she took action on behalf of her community, at a hundred-day vigil on behalf of Hurricane Maria victims in Union Square denouncing the government's treatment of Puerto Rico, for example, or a Black Lives Matter protest, she found that the members of the Democratic Socialists of America were there.

"When we talk about the word 'socialism,'" she says, "I think what it really means is just democratic participation in our economic dignity, and our economic, social, and racial dignity. It is about direct representation and people actually having power and stake over their economic and social wellness, at the end of the day. To me, what socialism means is to guarantee a basic level of dignity."

A number of American allies are democratic socialist societies—France, Brazil, Denmark, Finland, Germany, Greenland, Iceland, Norway, the Netherlands, Portugal, and Sweden to name a few.

Alexandria had backed Bernie Sanders, a democratic socialist himself, but she grew more comfortable with the party when she visited a DSA meeting in the basement of a church in Washington Heights and heard a group of undocumented immigrants describe their experiences being exploited in the workplace. "They were talking about how they were working in these factories with no windows, and they were being made to operate heavy machinery with no training, and that they were being paid far, far below anything that resembles a living wage," she told *Insider* magazine. She realized then that the DSA was interested in hearing the voices of the people. That's the kind of party she wanted to belong to, not one that was full of pollsters and spin doctors, and millionaires who did not know anything about the people they served. The current Democratic Party had done some great things, including the ACA and pushing back against Trump's agenda, but the American people needed more.

AOC wants many of the same things as the rest of the

Democrats, but she also represents the future of the party, and as a member of Congress, she's shaking things up. Americans were working hard and falling behind. She wanted to belong to a party that heard their voices, that sought to represent the struggling and underserved, the oppressed and dispossessed, and she found that willingness in those DSA meetings.

Still, she understands the importance of bringing new people to her point of view with kindness. Overall, as she told *Vogue*, she doesn't want to be pigeonholed. "I think it's real bougie to grow up with a defined political ideology. You need to have college-educated parents for that, with a political lexicon. My mother doesn't even have an English lexicon! When people say I'm not Socialist enough, I find that very classist. It's like, 'What—I didn't read enough books for you, buddy?'"

The DSA is growing, with more millennials joining in every election, inspired by Sen. Bernie Sanders and Rep. Rashida Tlaib. Between 2015 and 2017, the DSA grew from eight thousand dues-paying members to twenty-five thousand. During that time the average age of the group's members dropped from sixty-four to thirty. Its membership surged the day after Trump was elected and again the day after Ocasio-Cortez won her primary. By early 2020, it was fifty-five thousand members strong.

"[Socialism is] asserting the value of saying that the America we want and the America that we are proud of is one in which all children can access a dignified education," says AOC. "It's one in which no person is too poor to have the medicines they need to live. It's to say that no individual's civil rights are to be violated. And it's also to say that we need to really examine the historical inequities that have created much of the inequalities—both in terms of economics and social and racial justice—because they are intertwined."

THE FUTURE

Huh, because I'm happy
Clap along if you feel like a room without a roof.
—Pharrell Williams, "Happy"

By October 2019, there were eleven to thirteen people lacing up to run against Alexandria Ocasio-Cortez. Hahaha! Oh *puh-lease.* There was even a Republican in the mix, even though that district hadn't had a Republican in office for fifty years (remember, the general election in 2018 was basically a formality for AOC—winning the primary was the big deal). Yet, their hope lay in trying to capitalize on AOC's critics calling her too radical. Uh, good luck to those challengers. AOC's commitment to her constituents has made her a beloved representative in the district, and they'll continue to show up for her.

And that's how a queen knows she's really done something.

AOC's celebrity grew so *lit*, with followers in the millions, that her endorsement of Bernie Sanders gave *him* a boost during his 2020 primary campaign. Alexandria has done things differently since they opened those hallowed halls of Congress to her, and the goal is to have more queens like her enter. The lessons that she's already taught future candidates are important. Listen up: If you're intimidated, don't run away, embrace it—fight back.

AOC has never been shy about a fight. She does not back down when met with a problem; she'll see you in the battle. She's a kindhearted congresswoman, too, remember that, but, girls, don't be too sweet, she's both criticized and admired by fellow party members for her clap back. It's not about what people think, just clap back! Her tactics are to call a spade a spade, call a sexist, racist, and xenophobic president by his names too. Most important, what she has to pass on is the very life-changing magic of not giving a f**k about Fox News. *Hail the queen!* She will call them out on calling her out. Unlike many politicians, she's young and fun, but if the GOP attack her, her family, or the citizens of the United States of America, in about thirty seconds she will turn their attacks into a meme and send them into a viral pit.

And #SheReady for Trump any day, any year. His cheap shots don't cost her a thang; they only make her base stronger. They'll only get her reelected. The Right have tried all types of buffoonery to get AOC out or displaced, but they only make her followers love her more. Call her radical, call

ALEXANDRIA
THE
GREAT

her courageous, AOC does more than lean in on diversity, queens, she calls the shots.

When asked whether she'd ever want to run for president, she said, "Never. I want to be Bernie Sanders but never run for president. I want to be the kooky old lady who brings her cats to the floor of Congress and says, 'Here's the right thing to do.' I just want to be chilling with Sonia Sotomayor, wearing gold hoop earrings with a big old FU and a pretty necklace."

It would be pretty cool if someone like her ran for president, but you've got to respect a queen who knows what she wants. And, of course, running for president isn't the only or even the best way for a person to change the world for the better. No matter what the future holds for her, she's already a trailblazer, and politics will never be the same.

ACKNOWLEDGMENTS

Our agent, Johanna Castillo, at Writers House, is a true Queen of the Resistance and must go at the top of our acknowledgments. Wow, she is the very definition of love, creativity, and strength. We absolutely would not have had this opportunity without her strong vision and ability to keep us in check to get it done. We adore and honor you, queen. You are a changemaker who made our lifelong dreams of being published authors come true. Anytime you call us to have tea in your kitchen, we'll be there ASAP.

Thank you to the wonderful team at Plume who believed in this four-book series to celebrate these Queens of the Resistance. Special acknowledgments, high fives, dabs, and e-hugs to our brilliant, kind, and badass queen editors, Jill Schwartzman and Marya Pasciuto, and to the Plume team, who kept up the strong sisterhood and encouragement through and through to get this project done! *Yes, we can!* Thank you to the queens: Amanda Walker, Jamie Knapp, Becky Odell, Katie Taylor, Caroline Payne, Leila Siddiqui, Tiffany Estreicher, Alice Dalrymple, LeeAnn Pemberton, Susan Schwartz, Kaitlin Kall, and Dora Mak—and there were two good-guy allies who need a special shout-out, editor in chief John Parsley, and creative director Christopher Lin. To our publisher, Christine Ball, a strong woman and leader from the moment we met her, we especially love the army you've built and the work that you continue to innovate. Thank you!

THANK YOU, THANK YOU, THANK YOU (in all caps) to our beloved Ava Williams, our research assistant. You didn't know what you were getting yourself into, LOL, but your positive vibes and hard work held it up the entire time from beginning to end. Thank you for your warm and patient spirit throughout the process.

THANK YOU, THANK YOU, THANK YOU (in all caps again) to the talented Jonell Joshua for your beautiful images and being a creative who could make it through all the deadlines with precision. You're the best, girlfriend!

Krishan would like to give a big shout-out to her personal sister circle, the women in her life who took the lead in helping with Bleu on those daylong playdates: my sister, Dominique Marie Bell, Raven Brown-Walters, Renee Brown-Walters, Lenica Gomez, and Zaira Vasco. Special thanks to my crew at WeInspire—JLove, Brea Baker, and Taylor Shaw—and also to my mentors who guide me, especially Adrienne Ingrum, who has been a wonderful fountain of knowledge and inspiration throughout my path. This is for my mom, a Queen of the Resistance from Brooklyn and the Bronx, New York, who left us too soon but whom I felt watching over me from heaven smiling; and her twin, my loving auntie Amina Samad, who always came over with love and hugs to help throughout the process—I love and cherish you both so very much. Thank you to my son, Xavier Bleu Jeune, for being such an awesome growing boy. I love being #BleusMom. My favorite moment in this journey was when you said you wanted to be a "comedic author" (not to be confused with author, *okay*). I love you. And last but never least, thank you to my copilot, Brenda, for rockin' this out with me!

Brenda would like to thank her friends on Capitol Hill; without your passion and determination to fight legislatively and strategically in this hard time, our democracy might no longer exist. My struggle for you here was to incline this project toward a true representation of your sacrifice, intellect, and capability. To special friends who helped me hang in there: Kathryn Williams, Cheryl Johnson, Shashrina Thomas, Ingrid Gavin-Parks, Kim Ross, Michael Hagbourne, Joan Kelsey, and the DMV Quartet. Thanks to Bernard Demczuk for opening the Growlery at Giverny West whenever I needed quiet concentration. To the absolute best parents—the late Myrtle Bowers Davis and Robert Lee Davis—who instilled in me the highest integrity, the best education, and the richest experiences. To Rep. John Lewis, without whom my career in politics would never have been possible. Thank you for your unwavering faith in me and unyielding commitment to art, inspiration, creativity, justice, and peace.

Thanks to Speaker Nancy Pelosi, Chairwoman Maxine Waters, Sen. Elizabeth Warren, and Rep. Alexandria Ocasio-Cortez for your bright, shining lives of public service. Krishan, Plume, and I can only hope that we have begun to return to you just a small part of what you sacrifice so much to give to us all. Hail the Queens of the Resistance.

To our readers, from our hearts to yours, *thank you*, *thank you*, *thank you* for celebrating the Queens of the Resistance series with us!

SOURCES

Acosta-Belén, Dr. Edna. "Brief Historical Chronology of Puerto Ricans in the United States (Part IV)." The Center for Puerto Rican Studies, Puerto Rican Heritage Poster Series, 2013.

Ainsley, Julia, and Jacob Soboroff. "Agents Feared Riots, Armed Themselves Because of Dire Conditions at Migrant Facility, DHS Report Says." NBCNews.com, July 1, 2019. https://www.nbc news.com/politics/immigration/dhs-warned-may-border -station-conditions-so-bad-agents-feared-n1025136.

Aleksander, Irina. "How Alexandria Ocasio-Cortez and Other Progressives Are Defining the Midterms." *Vogue*, October 15, 2018.

American Civil Liberties Union. "Fighting Cuts to Voting Access." Accessed February 29, 2020, https://www.aclu.org/issues/vot ing-rights/fighting-voter-suppression/fighting-cuts-voting -access.

Andrews-Dyer, Helena. "Reliable Source: Alexandria Ocasio-Cortez's Mom Wants Her to Get Married—And Yes, She Has a Boyfriend." *Washington Post*, March 5, 2019.

Atler, Charlotte, and Alana Abramson. "The Making of AOC." *Time*, April 1, 2019.

Berry, Michael. "Ocasio-Cortez Says NY Democrats Engaged in Voter Suppression in Primary." KTRH Radio, August 8, 2019.

Brockes, Emma. "When Alexandria Ocasio-Cortez Met Greta Thunberg." *Guardian*, June 29, 2019.

Bryant, Miranda. "Four Restaurants in the Bronx Feel the Alexandria Ocasio-Cortez Effect." *Guardian*, June 24, 2019.

Buncombe, Andrew. "AOC Denounces ICE as 'Rogue Agency' After Visit to 'Unsafe' Child Detention Centre." *Independent*, July 2, 2019.

C-SPAN. "House Session." Accessed February 29, 2020, https://www.c-span.org/video/?456929-2/237-187-house-passes-121-billion-disaster-relief-bill-february-8.

Cadigan, Hillary. "Alexandria Ocasio-Cortez Learned Her Most Important Lessons from Restaurants." *Bon Appétit*, November 7, 2018.

Cochrane, Emily. "Lawmakers Criticize Migrant Holding Sites as 'Toxic' and 'Broken.'" *New York Times*, July 2, 2019.

Colón, Ana. "Rep. Alexandria Ocasio-Cortez Wore a Cape to the 2019 State of the Union." *Glamour*, February 6, 2019.

Congresswoman Alexandria Ocasio-Cortez. "Criminal Justice Reform." Accessed February 17, 2020, https://ocasio-cortez.house.gov/issues/criminal-justice-reform.

———. "Economic Inequality." Accessed February 17, 2020, https://ocasio-cortez.house.gov/issues/economic-inequality.

———. "Education." Accessed February 17, 2020, https://ocasio-cortez.house.gov/issues/education.

———. "Green New Deal." Accessed February 17, 2020, https://ocasio-cortez.house.gov/gnd.

———. "Gun Control." Accessed February 17, 2020, https://oca sio-cortez.house.gov/issues/gun-control.

———. "Healthcare." Accessed February 17, 2020, https://ocasio -cortez.house.gov/issues/health.

———. "Housing." Accessed February 17, 2020, https://ocasio -cortez.house.gov/issues/housing.

———. "Immigration." Accessed February 17, 2020, https://ocasio -cortez.house.gov/issues/immigration.

———. "LGBTQIA + Rights." Accessed February 17, 2020, https:// ocasio-cortez.house.gov/issues/lgbtqia-rights.

———. "Reproductive Justice." Accessed February 18, 2020, https://ocasio-cortez.house.gov/issues/reproductive-justice.

———. "Solidarity with Puerto Rico." Accessed February 18, 2020, https://ocasio-cortez.house.gov/issues/solidarity-puerto-rico.

Cottle, Michelle. "In the Squad, Mr. Trump Finds His Foil." *The New York Times*, July 17, 2019.

Denvir, Daniel. "Alexandria Ocasio-Cortez, in Her Own Words." *Jacobin*, July 11, 2018.

DeSantis, Rachel. "Alexandria Ocasio-Cortez Remembers Dad's Rare Cancer Diagnosis and How Their Family 'Almost Lost Our Home.'" *People*, July 31, 2019.

Doctorow, Cory. "AOC Grills Pharma Exec About Why the HIV-Prevention Drug Prep Costs $8 in Australia Costs $1,780 in the USA." *BoingBoing*, May 18, 2019.

Dorman, Sam. "In Netflix Doc, AOC Reflects on 2018 Run: 'Nobody Else Would, So Literally Anybody Could.'" Fox News, May 2, 2019, https://www.foxnews.com/entertainment/in-net flix-doc-aoc-reflects-on-2018-run-nobody-else-would-so-lite rally-anybody-could.

Farmer, Brit McCandless. "More from Rep. Alexandria Ocasio-Cortez on *60 Minutes*." CBS News, January 6, 2019.

Farzan, Antonia Noori. "'The 2018 Version of Fireside Chats': People Can't Get Enough of Watching Alexandria Ocasio-Cortez Make Soup on Instagram." *Washington Post*, November 20, 2018.

Fisher, Jason, Denis Slattery, and Chris Sommerfeldt. "AOC Calls Out Cuomo, State Dems over 'Horrifying' Voting Laws After Cabán's Concession in Queens DA Race." *Daily News*, August 8, 2019.

Friedman, Lisa. "Kamala Harris and Alexandria Ocasio-Cortez Release Climate 'Equity Plan.'" *New York Times*, July 29, 2019.

Gallucci, Nicole. "7 of Alexandria Ocasio-Cortez's most Inspirational Speeches." Mashable.com, March 27, 2019.

Goldmacher, Shane. "He Had Power and Loaded Campaign War Chest, but It Wasn't Enough." *New York Times*, June 28, 2018.

Goodkind, Nicole. "Chris Christie Lets Loose on Alexandria Ocasio-Cortez, Ivanka and Jared, 2020 and . . . Meatloaf." *Newsweek*, February 15, 2019.

Harrison, Olivia. "How to Snack Like Alexandria Ocasio-Cortez." *Refinery29*, January 16, 2019.

Hendrickson, Mark. "The Alexandria Ocasio-Cortez Phenomenon." *Epoch Times*, January 29, 2019.

Hess, Abigail. "Alexandria Ocasio-Cortez Says She Paid Twice as Much for Insurance as a Waitress as She Will in Congress." CNBC, December 4, 2018.

Holmes, Helen. "Alexandria Ocasio-Cortez Is Quoting Cardi B on Twitter, and We're Here for It." *Observer*, November 20, 2018.

Inskeep, Steve. "N.Y. Rep. Alexandria Ocasio-Cortez on How the Democratic Party Is Evolving." *All Things Considered*, NPR Transcript, February 6, 2019.

Independent. "'Horrifying' Conditions of US Migrant Camps Exposed." July 3, 2019.

International Business Times. "Alexandria Ocasio-Cortez May Have Illegally Paid Boyfriend During Campaign." March 2, 2019.

John, Arit. "Making Room for a New Squad." *New York Times*, July 21, 2019.

Karl, Jonathan. "One-on-One with Rep. Alexandria-Ocasio-Cortez." *This Week*, ABC News Transcript, June 16, 2019.

Kelly, Caroline. "Ocasio-Cortez Defends Impeachment Inquiry as Preventing 'Potential Meddling in the 2020 Election That Has Still Yet to Happen.'" CNN, September 26, 2019.

Kurtzleben, Danielle. "Rep. Alexandria Ocasio-Cortez Releases Green New Deal Outline." *All Things Considered*, NPR Transcript, February 7, 2019.

Library of Congress. "Immigration . . . Puerto Rican/Cuban." Accessed February 29, 2020, https://www.loc.gov/teachers/class roommaterials/presentationsandactivities/presentations/immig ration/cuban4.html.

Lipsitz, Raina. "What's Next for AOC?" *Nation*, October 29, 2018.

Lyons, Joseph D. "Alexandria Ocasio-Cortez's Women's March Speech Calls for Turning Power into Policy." *Bustle*, January 20, 2019.

Madhani, Aamer. "AOC, Sanders Want to Cap Credit Card Interest." *USA Today*, May 10, 2019.

Mays, Jeffery C. "Ocasio-Cortez Is Also Sued for Blocking Twitter Users." *New York Times*, July 11, 2019.

McDonald, Scott. "ICE Chief Rips Alexandria Ocasio-Cortez Comment Comparing Detention Facilities to Concentration Camps." *Newsweek*, June 18, 2019.

Minsberg, Talya. "How Alexandria Ocasio-Cortez Is Bringing Her Instagram Followers into the Political Process." *New York Times*, November 16, 2018.

Moran, Lee. "Alexandria Ocasio-Cortez and Elizabeth Warren Breathe Dragon Fire on 'Game of Thrones' Finale." *Huffington Post*, May 22, 2019.

Morris, Alex. "Alexandria Ocasio-Cortez Wants the Country to Think Big." *Rolling Stone*, March 2019.

NHI Magazine. "Alexandria-Ocasio-Cortez Named 2017 NHI Person of the Year." December 31, 2017.

Nichols, John. "'I Want Us to Be That Party Again': An Interview with Alexandria Ocasio-Cortez." *The Progressive*, October–November 2018.

———. "The AOC Effect." *Nation*, September 10, 2018.

ObamaCare Facts. "What Is ObamaCare?" Accessed February 29, 2020, https://obamacarefacts.com/whatis-obamacare/.

Ocasio-Cortez, Alexandria (@AOC). "The Restaurant I Used to Work at Is Closing Its Doors." Twitter, August 20, 2018, 1:42 p.m. Accessed February 18, 2020, https://twitter.com/AOC/status/1031597371061411841.

Ocasio-Cortez, Gabriel (@gabecortez). "I Nominated the Best Person for the Job, She Just Happened to Be My Sister." Twitter. May 30, 2019. Accessed February 17, 2020, https://twitter.com/gabecortez/status/1134130701140398080.

———. "For the Record I Will Always Be Proud of the Country That Elected My Amazing Sister to Congress." Twitter. July 14,

2019. Accessed February 17, 2020, https://twitter.com/gabe cortez/status/1150537519433474053.

O'Keefe, Ed, and Margaret Brennan, "Interview with New York Congressional Candidate Alexandria Ocasio-Cortez." *Face the Nation*, July 22, 2018.

Paiella, Gabriella. "The 28-Year-Old at the Center of One of This Year's Most Exciting Primaries." *The Cut*, June 25, 2018.

Quinn, Liam. "Rep. Alexandria Ocasio-Cortez Attacks ICE as a Dangerous Agency." Fox News, March 2, 2019.

Read, Bridget. "36 Hours with Alexandria Ocasio-Cortez." *Vogue*, June 28, 2019.

Relevant. "AOC: After Standing Rock Protest I Prayed, 'Lord Do With Me What You Will.'" January 21, 2020.

Relman, Eliza. "The Story of How Democratic Rising Stars Alexandria Ocasio-Cortez and Ayanna Pressley First Met at a Manhattan House Party and Became 'BFFs.'" *Business Insider*, January 7, 2019.

———. "The Truth About Alexandria Ocasio Cortez: The Inside Story of How, in Just One Year, Sandy the Bartender Became a Lawmaker Who Triggers Both Parties." *Insider*, January 6, 2019.

Remnick, David. "Alexandria Ocasio-Cortez's Historic Win and the Future of the Democratic Party." *New Yorker*, July 16, 2018.

———. "Left Wing of the Possible." *New Yorker*, July 23, 2018.

Renae, Merle. "Alexandria Ocasio-Cortez vs. Wall Street: Lawmaker Wins Spot on Powerful House Committee." *Washington Post*, January 16, 2019.

Robin, Marci. "Like Me, Alexandria Ocasio-Cortez Enjoys a $8 Press-On Manicure with a Nice Glass of Wine." *Allure*, January 15, 2019.

Rodulfo, Kristina. "Alexandria Ocasio-Cortez Details Her Skincare Routine and Offers Tips on Oration in the Same IG Story." *Elle*, January 28, 2019.

Ryzik, Melena. "'Ugly Crying' Along Paths to Power." *New York Times*, May 6, 2019.

Schwarz, Hunter. "Alexandria Ocasio-Cortez's First Month in Congress: A List." CNN, February 3, 2019.

Scott, Sherrie. "What Are the Consequences of Not Having Health Insurance?" Sapling.com, Accessed February 29, 2020, https://www.sapling.com/5549791/consequences-not-having-health-insurance.

Shannon, Joel. "Old Alexandria Ocasio-Cortez Dance Video Goes Viral as Supporters Mock Shaming Attempt." *USA Today*, January 3, 2019.

Shapiro, Emily. "5 Natural Disasters That Devastated the US in 2018." ABC News, December 8, 2018.

Silverstein, Jason. "Who Is 'the Squad'? What You Need to Know About Ocasio-Cortez, Omar, Pressley and Tlaib." CBS News, July 16, 2019.

Smith, David. "Alexandria Ocasio-Cortez Says She'd Be 'Hard Pressed' to Back Biden in Primary; Bernie Sanders Appears to Be the Favorite to Secure Ocasio-Cortez's Prized Endorsement in the Democratic Presidential Primary." *Guardian*, May 22, 2019.

Stolberg, Sheryl Gay. "'Squad' Rankles, but Pelosi and Ocasio-Cortez Make Peace for Now." *New York Times*, July 27, 2019.

Thebault, Reis. "Conservatives Can't Stop Obsessing over Ocasio-Cortez. Their Latest Target: Her Boyfriend." *Washington Post*, February 16, 2019.

United States Congress. "H.R.6—American Dream and Promise Act of 2019." Accessed February 29, 2020, https://www.cong ress.gov/bill/ 116th-congress/house-bill/6.

———. "Representative Alexandria Ocasio-Cortez." Accessed February 29, 2020, https://www.congress.gov/member/Alexandria -ocasiocortez/O000172.

———. "S.874—Dream Act of 2019." Accessed February 29, 2020, https://www.congress.gov/bill/116th-congress/senate-bill /874.

Valenti, Lauren. "Alexandria Ocasio-Cortez Reveals Her Multistep Skin-Care Routine on Instagram." *Vogue*, January 28, 2019.

Warren, Elizabeth. "Alexandria Ocasio-Cortez." *Time*, April 29, 2019/May 6, 2019.

ABOUT THE AUTHORS

Brenda Jones is best known for her fifteen-year tenure as communications director for an icon of American politics, Rep. John Lewis. All of his published opinions, statements, and speeches, ranging from his introductions of US presidents to commencement addresses delivered to the Ivy League, and those celebrating his transformative Civil Rights legacy were penned by Brenda Jones during that time. She collaborated with him on his book, *Across That Bridge: A Vision for Change and the Future of America*, which won an NAACP Image Award. She has also worked in commercial television news and public broadcasting.

Krishan Trotman is an executive editor at Hachette Books, recently profiled in *Essence* magazine as one of the few African American publishing executives. She has committed over fifteen years to publishing books by and about multicultural voices and social justice. Throughout her career as an editor she has proudly worked with leaders and trailblazers on this frontier such as John Lewis, Stephanie Land, Malcolm Nance, Zerlina Maxwell, Mika Brzezinski, Al Roker, Ryan Serhant, and Lindy West.